DON EASTWOOD 1.24/82

D-DAY

D-DAY

BRIGADIER PETER YOUNG

A Bison Book

CONTENTS

First published in the US by
Galahad Books
a division of A&W Publishers, Inc.
95 Madison Avenue
New York
New York 10016

Produced by
Bison Books Limited
4 Cromwell Place
London SW7

Library of Congress Catalog Card Number:
81-80459

ISBN 0-88365-551-9

Printed in Hong Kong

Page 1: Troops coming ashore during a training exercise for D-Day.
Page 2–3: One of the German coastal batteries carries out a practice shoot.
Page 4–5: A scene on Omaha Beach shortly after the first landings.

1. PREPARING FOR INVASION

On 6 June 1944, in the greatest combined operation of all time, the Allies assaulted the strongly fortified coast of France, broke through the defenses and secured a lodgment. This, with the battle for Normandy that followed, must rank among the decisive battles of the world.

The assault was made at a time when the Germans were already fighting for their lives on the Eastern Front and when the Allies had already won mastery of both air and sea. Even so the result was far from being a foregone conclusion. The Allied troops who took part, though fairly well trained, were not for the most part very experienced. If the Allied leaders had proved their skill in former campaigns, the same must also be said of the German leaders, von Rundstedt and Rommel. However, the Allies had built up a remarkable partnership. Cooperation between the Americans and the British was close and efficient, and if this account emphasizes the part played by the two main Allies, it must be remembered that the Canadians, French, Poles, Belgians, Dutch, Czechs and the Yugoslavs all played a valiant part in the ultimate victory.

The Allies owed their success in large measure to the skills they had developed in the techniques of amphibious warfare. The British Combined Operations Headquarters had set new standards in interservice cooperation, masterminded by Lord Louis Mountbatten.

Allied industrial capacity ensured that their forces went into battle well armed and well equipped. Wars are won by fighting

Top left: Field Marshal Erwin Rommel during a tour of inspection of the Atlantic Wall defenses in spring 1944.
Top right: Rommel's immediate superior in 1944 was Field Marshal von Rundstedt.
Left: A German machine-gun section covers a potential landing beach on the invasion coast.

men; morale is even more important than weaponry. The campaigns in Sicily and Italy in 1943, allowed the Germans to demonstrate the skill and determination which had won them their great victories of the 1939–41 period. How would the young Allied warrior measure up to the German soldier of 1944? That was the question.

The Allies had made no secret of their intention to invade Europe, and as early as 1942 there had been a great deal of ill-informed pressure for a 'Second Front Now!' Sympathy for the Soviets and sheer ignorance of the Allies' unpreparedness contributed to this clamor. It has been argued that the invasion should have been launched in the summer of 1943, but few if any of those who held responsible positions on the Allied side were of that opinion at the time. When the blow eventually fell, the Germans had been preparing their defenses for the better part of four years.

The task of repelling the invasion fell to Field Marshal Karl Rudolf Gerd von Rundstedt, who in March 1942 was recalled from retirement for the second time and appointed Commander in Chief, West. His responsibilities included the defense of France, Belgium and Holland, the countries where the Allies were expected to launch their assault. He was answerable only to the Führer himself.

On 23 March 1942, in Directive No 40, Hitler laid down the defensive policy by which he intended to foil any Allied attack. Fortified areas were to be prepared in coastal sectors exposed to a landing, and reserves were to be held ready for a counterattack. It was laid down that 'enemy forces which have landed must be destroyed or thrown back into the sea by immediate counterattack.'

Von Rundstedt had scarcely assumed command when, on 28 March, the British carried out a fierce raid on the naval base of St Nazaire. The great dock was put out of action, and Hitler, greatly displeased, ordered the construction of yet more formidable defenses. The results of the British and Canadian raid on Dieppe on 19 August confirmed the Führer's good opinion of the value of coastal fortifications. Von Rundstedt, for his part, believed in the more conventional strategy of a strong *masse de manoeuvre*, held well back, but

capable of launching a massive counterattack against an Allied beachhead.

Von Rundstedt was the supreme example of the orthodox general of the Prussian school. A little old fashioned perhaps, he was nonetheless the man given the credit for having struck down France in the Blitzkrieg of 1940. From there he had gone on to the Soviet Union, but blunt criticism of the Führer's strategy had led to his replacement. He was greatly respected by the German officer corps, which helped him in his dealings with Hitler. He had a low opinion of his master – though he had the wit to conceal it. His new job had its consolations; he enjoyed a civilized life at his headquarters in the Château de St Germain-en-Laye, overlooking the Seine. He needed something to make up for a task which he himself was to describe thus:

'I had over 3000 miles of coastline to cover from the Italian frontier in the south to the German frontier in the north, and only 60 divisions with which to defend it. Most of them were low-grade divisions and some of them were skeletons.'

Well versed in military history, von Rundstedt was familiar with Frederick the Great's dictum, 'Little minds want to defend everything; sensible men concentrate on the essential.' What were the essentials and if he should succeed in selecting them, would Hitler let him develop his strategy unhindered? During 1943 it became evident that the answer to this last question was an emphatic no. Hitler was growing more nervous. General Gunther Blumentritt commented:

'He was constantly on the jump – at one moment he expected an invasion in Norway, at another in Holland, then near the Somme, or Normandy or Brittany, in Portugal, in Spain, in the Adriatic.'

At the tactical level the task of defending the Channel coast fell to Field Marshal Erwin Rommel, an officer of outstanding tactical skill. Rommel felt that 'the war will be won or lost on the beaches. The first 24 hours will be decisive.' Unfortunately for the Germans his ideas did not entirely coincide with those of von Rundstedt, upon whom the ultimate responsibility rested.

Rommel, unlike so many of the German generals, could boast no aristocratic origins. He was the son of a Bavarian schoolmaster. Commissioned in 1912 he had distinguished himself greatly in World War I, at platoon, company and battle group level. He had fought in turn against the French, the Rumanians and the Italians, always with outstanding success. Skill, courage, vigor and initiative were the hallmarks of his operations. His decorations included the highest, the Pour le Mérite. Rommel was fortunate in that his battle experience was not confined to the trench warfare of the Western Front. He did not belong to the school of thought which believed in limited advances following a barrage. His exploits in Rumania and Italy had shown him the value of speed and surprise to achieve deep penetration of an enemy position.

Rommel stayed on in the small army allowed to Germany by the Treaty of Versailles, rising to the rank of colonel, and commanding the Führer's bodyguard in the Sudetenland and in Poland in 1939. Convinced of the value of the tank in modern warfare, he asked for the command of an armored division, and was given 7th Panzer, which he led with notable élan in the Blitzkrieg of 1940. Thereafter his advancement was rapid for although Rommel was not a fanatical Nazi Hitler preferred him to the Prussian aristocrats, who had such a firm grip on the German General Staff.

In February 1941 Rommel, now a Lieutenant General, was sent to Libya, where the Italians had been roughly handled in the so-called Wavell Offensive. During the next 18 months he built up a tremendous reputation as a tank commander in desert warfare. His capture of Tobruk on 21 June 1942 won him the field marshal's baton, and a reputation for invincibility. However, Auchinleck held him at El Alamein, and Rommel found himself far from his base, starved of supplies and suffering from a stomach ailment. On 23 October, when Rommel was in hospital in Germany, a new British general, Montgomery, fell upon his army and broke it in the long and bitter battle of El Alamein.

Rommel's reputation survived the loss of North Africa, and, after a spell in Italy, he was sent to inspect the defenses of northern France in November 1943. At first Rommel had no direct responsibility, and he felt that this made him ineffectual. He complained to Berlin and was given command of Army Group B under von Rundstedt. Although this clarified the chain of command it also revealed the fundamental difference in outlook of the two field marshals.

Von Rundstedt believed in a powerful, mobile armored reserve, a *masse de manoeuvre*, which would move against the invaders wherever they might choose to land. This was, of course, excellent theory. The lack of such a reserve had paralyzed Gamelin in 1940. Rommel, the great exponent of mobile warfare, had a far

greater practical knowledge of handling tanks than von Rundstedt. Even so one might have supposed that his commander in chief's solution would have appealed to him. In fact Rommel had no faith in von Rundstedt's plan. It was not that he was abandoning the principles that had won him his desert successes. Practical tactician that he was, he simply appreciated that Allied air superiority would delay the armored reserve so much that it would rob it of its mobility. It would not be able to move quickly enough to prevent the Allies securing a foothold, building up a bridgehead and eventually achieving a breakout. Under all the circumstances Rommel felt that the only hope was to prevent the Allies landing at all; to stop them on the beaches. This meant that a thin gray line, supported by armor spread out close to the coastline, must be organized so as to hurl back the Allies on D-Day, as had been done at Dieppe in 1942.

In fact the plans of the two field marshals were never really reconciled. Von Rundstedt continued to sit on his mobile reserves, while Rommel sped up and down the coast, inspecting units and fortresses, siting guns, inventing obstacles and gingering up the defenders with his considerable powers of leadership. With the benefit of hindsight one must concede that, given Allied domination of the skies above Normandy, Rommel's plan was more realistic than von Rundstedt's, however correct that may have been in theory.

During the period of rather more than two years between von Rundstedt's appointment and D-Day the forces at his command suffered considerable erosion. Every time the Germans suffered a setback elsewhere Hitler nibbled away at von Rundstedt's armies until their quality became decidedly uneven. That is not to say that von Rundstedt did not still have formations of superb military value. No soldier worth the name would underrate the 10 Panzer divisions which formed the solid core of his forces.

One way of measuring the strength of Germany at the beginning of 1944 is simply to examine the layout of divisions in the field:

Eastern Front	179
France and the Low Countries	53
Balkan States	26
Italy	22
Scandinavia	16
Finland	8
	304

Of these, 24, stationed in the occupied countries, were still in the process of formation. Worse still, there was no general reserve in Germany. Hitler had a tremendous army at his command, but it was already committed. Only by robbing other fronts could he reinforce the West. Even

so, the occupation forces were formidable. In wartime the ration strength of an army tends to be a good deal higher than its real strength. Not *all* quartermasters are honest. However that may be, on 1 March 1944 there were in France:

Army	806,927
SS and Police	85,230
Volunteers (foreigners)	61,439
Allies	13,631
Air Force	337,140
Navy	96,084
Total	1,400,451
Armed Force Auxiliaries	145,611

Of the Air Force personnel over 100,000 were in Flak formations, and more than 30,000 were 'paratroops.' The Luftwaffe in the West under Field Marshal Hugo Sperrle had about 890 aircraft available for operations. Of these about 150 were reconnaissance and transport aircraft.

Vice-Admiral Krancke commanded Naval Group, West. Naval personnel manned a number of the key coastal batteries with radar equipment – thus complicating defense policy. The ships and craft available included a weak destroyer flotilla, some torpedo boats, a number of patrol craft and minelayers. There were U-Boats based at Brest, and other Atlantic coast ports, but they were not under Krancke. These, in broad terms were the forces the Allies had to reckon with.

At the last meeting of the Cairo Conference, on 6 December 1943, President Roosevelt nominated General Dwight

Above: A Freya early-warning radar sited to cover the approaches to Brest on the Channel coast.
Above right: Churchill and Roosevelt met at Quebec in August 1943 to discuss plans for the invasion of Western France.
Right: At Casablanca in January 1943 the British Prime Minister came under strong pressure from the Americans to launch a cross-Channel invasion in the near future.

David Eisenhower as Supreme Allied Commander for Operation Overlord. Before he took up his new appointment, as he generously conceded later, Lieutenant General Frederick E Morgan had already 'made D-Day possible.'

At the Casablanca Conference in January 1943 the Allies had decided to set up a Combined Allied Staff to plan Overlord. The Chief of Staff to the Supreme Allied Commander (designate), Morgan, was British, and his deputy, Major General Ray W Baker, was a United States army officer. The organization became known as COSSAC.

Morgan received his directive on 26 April 1943. This stated, 'our object is to defeat the German fighting forces in Northwest Europe.' It instructed COSSAC to prepare plans for a full-scale assault against the Continent as early as possible in 1944, with 'an elaborate camouflage and deception scheme' extending over the summer of 1943 designed to pin the Germans in the

west by keeping alive their expectation of an invasion that year. In the event of the Germans collapsing there was to be a plan ready so that whatever forces were available in the United Kingdom could immediately be sent to the Continent. At the Trident Conference, held in Washington in May 1943, the target date for Overlord was set for 1 May 1944. COSSAC was given a list of the forces which, it was thought, would be available:

5 infantry divisions in assault vessels
2 follow-up infantry divisions
2 airborne divisions
20 divisions for movement into the lodgment area.

The capture and development of ports would permit the landing of divisions direct from America, or elsewhere, at a rate of from three to five a month.

The assault of ships and landing craft would amount to some 3300. It seems a

huge figure, but in fact shortage of landing craft was to plague the Allies until the end of the war in Europe. About 11,400 aircraft, including 632 transport planes for airborne operations, would be available.

In the first week of June General Morgan was told to submit his outline plan by 1 August 1943. That he was able to do so was due to Winston Churchill's aggressive policy, which, even before Dunkirk, had called for raids on the enemy-held coast, and plans for an eventual return to France. The small organization under General A G B Bourne, Royal Marines, which in 1940 was charged with this task, had expanded under Admiral of the Fleet, Sir Roger Keyes. Later it expanded far more significantly under Vice-Admiral Mountbatten, whose Combined Operations Headquarters, though affiliated to the Admiralty, the War Office and the Air Ministry, was separate from them. Mountbatten, who held equivalent rank in all three services, sat as a member of the Chiefs of Staff

Committee. He was the recognized authority on the planning and mounting of seaborne assaults, whether commando raids or full-scale invasions. The zeal and originality which Mountbatten brought to Combined Operations Headquarters permeated through to the staff of all three services in the planning of Overlord.

At the Quadrant meeting in Quebec in August 1943 the COSSAC plan, after being considered in turn by the British Chiefs of Staff and the American Joint Chiefs of Staff was finally submitted to Churchill and Roosevelt by their Combined Chiefs of Staff. It was accepted, with some useful modifications. Churchill urged that the force should be increased by at least 25 percent and that the assault front should be extended to include the eastern coast of the Cherbourg peninsula. The Combined Chiefs, although they agreed that the force should be strengthened if possible, did not

increase the allocation of ships and craft.

General Morgan was now given authority 'for taking the necessary executive action to implement those plans approved by the Combined Chiefs of Staff.' Since nearly four months were to pass before Eisenhower's appointment Morgan was working as Chief of Staff to an unknown Supreme Commander. All that was known was that, at Churchill's suggestion, he was to be an American, since the United States would eventually be providing a larger proportion of the Allied force.

Eisenhower was an admirable choice for Supreme Commander, not by virtue of battle experience in World War I – he had none – nor outstanding strategic skill, but because his lack of personal ambition, his sincere, warm and friendly personality fitted him to run a team which included such idiosyncratic characters as Patton and Montgomery. Son of a Texan railroad

Above: General Dwight D Eisenhower was appointed Supreme Commander of the Allied Expeditionary Force in December 1943.
Below: German coastal artillery was sited in concrete emplacements overlooking potential landing beaches.

worker, he was brought up in poverty, but won his way to West Point, and was commissioned in 1913. He served under the great General Douglas MacArthur in the Philippines, and later attracted the attention of General George C Marshall, who was Roosevelt's principal military adviser throughout the war. Eisenhower was hardly of the caliber of either of these giants, but he was an excellent chairman, and enjoyed great popularity with the British.

As Deputy Supreme Commander a British Air Chief Marshal, Sir Arthur Tedder, was chosen. He had already worked harmoniously with Eisenhower in 1943 when he had been Commander in Chief, Mediterranean Allied Air Forces. His success in planning and executing operations over Tunisia, Sicily and Italy made him an excellent choice, for it was evident that the air arm would be of paramount importance in the campaign ahead. Eisenhower con-

sidered him 'one of the few great military leaders of our time.' A Luftwaffe comment of the time is flattering:

'Tedder is on good terms with Eisenhower to whom he is superior in both intelligence and energy. The coming operations will be conducted by him to a very large extent. . . . Obviously we are dealing here with one of the most eminent personalities among the invasion leaders.'

Not unnaturally Eisenhower wished to retain his trusted Chief of Staff, Lieutenant General W Bedell Smith, who had been with him in North Africa, Sicily and Italy. Although he was Eisenhower's hatchet man, he could be diplomatic as well as tough. Morgan, whose knowledge of how the COSSAC plan had developed was invaluable, became a deputy chief of staff.

The naval commander was Admiral Sir

Bertram Ramsay, the man who brought the British Expeditionary Force (BEF) home from the beaches of Dunkirk. He had helped to plan the landings in North Africa in 1942, and had commanded the Eastern Naval Task Force in the assault on Sicily. He was a punctilious man who believed in attention to detail – there are enough hazards at sea without leaving things to chance when you do not have to. Nevertheless some of the American admirals were to be critical of the amount of detail in his orders. Ramsay remained calm and urbane.

Command of the Allied Tactical Air Forces was given to Air Chief Marshal Sir Trafford Leigh-Mallory who, like Ramsay, had special qualifications for his role. After commanding 12 Group in the Battle of Britain, he had been the Air Force commander of the Royal Air Force School of Army Cooperation, and Air Officer Commanding in Chief, Fighter Command. He

Left: A German sentry keeps watch from a camouflaged observation post. Allied measures against German radar were so successful that these lookouts provided the first warning of invasion.

was prepared to stand up to 'the bomber barons.'

Command of the Allied Armies, 21st Army Group, was given to General Sir Bernard Montgomery. Eisenhower wanted to have General Sir Harold Alexander, but the British government knew that the victor of El Alamein could not be lightly set aside. In any case Alexander had all the qualities required to run the very mixed team of Allies then slogging their way up Italy. So it fell to Montgomery to command the land forces in Overlord. He was a strange man, not really very likeable, though he had sufficient sense of humor to be amused by his own peculiarities, which, besides a brusque manner, included a direct line to the Almighty. Although he got on badly with some colleagues – Patton for one detested him – he had an almost magical influence on the British soldier. When Montgomery was in command the men thought they could not be beaten. Though a strong-minded, efficient, sound and relentless commander, it cannot be said that he was especially gifted as a strategist. However, in the spring of 1944 his chief reverse, at Arnhem, still lay in the future. Thus far his road had been strewn with laurels. Had he not routed the great Rommel himself?

Command of the American First Army, which was one of the two assault armies, was in the safe hands of Lieutenant General Omar N Bradley. Commissioned in 1915, Bradley was made Lieutenant Colonel only in 1936, when he was already 43. During World War II promotion came rapidly, and in Tunisia and Sicily he had been a corps commander. He and Eisenhower had been friends since their West Point days, and the latter wrote of Bradley's 'ability and reputation as a sound, painstaking, and broadly educated soldier.' The newspapermen, led by Ernie Pyle, took a liking to him, and he became 'the GIs' general.'

The follow-up army of this group, the 12th Army Group, was the United States Third Army, under the dynamic and talented Lieutenant General George S Patton. His army took no part in the D-Day landing but its very existence was another worry for von Rundstedt.

The assault army of the 21st Army Group was the British Second Army, whose commander, Lieutenant General Sir Miles Dempsey, had commanded a corps in Sicily and Italy. He was an exceptionally fine commander, but unlike most of his contemporaries he left no memoirs and is therefore comparatively little-known today. He was good-tempered, steady, confident and considerate, and was tremendously respected by all who knew him. He had a perfect understanding of the army he handled, and had the knack of giving clear and precise verbal orders. Above all he had the ability to work with Montgomery, apparently without the least friction. Taken all round Dempsey was just about the ideal commander for the Second Army. Many a

British general of far less worth has ended his career with a field marshal's baton in his hand!

The First Canadian Army, under Lieutenant General Henry D G Crerar was the follow-up army of the 21st Army Group. It did not become operational until 23 July, but nevertheless its very existence had to be taken into account by the Germans.

In a sense the Allies already had an army in Europe before D-Day, the Resistance. In theory the constitutional government was the Vichy regime under old Marshal Pétain. His authority had been greatly reduced and Pierre Laval, who secured the collaboration which the Germans demanded, governed only by their consent. By 1944 it was clear that the true voice of France was that of General Charles de Gaulle, whose Headquarters was, of course, in London.

The French Resistance has been called 'a blend of courage and patriotism, ambition, faction and treachery.' It comprised numerous groups, whose political background varied from Communist and *Front Populaire* to Catholic. By 1944 the Maquis consisted of perhaps 100,000 people, many of whom had made their way to the mountains rather than be sent to Germany to work as conscript labor. They were the raw material for guerrilla war.

The Belgian Resistance, the 'Secret Army,' was some 45,000 strong. In the second quarter of 1944 55 air operations supplied it with arms. However, the *Abwehr* (German secret service) had been extremely successful in capturing Allied agents dropped into Holland, and the Dutch Resistance was still poorly equipped.

A complicated organization in England endeavored to control and to arm these Resistance movements. In this work the British Broadcasting Corporation and the Special Operations Executive (SOE) played an indispensable part.

The Allied planners, while agreeing that the flames of resistance must be fanned by every possible means, placed no reliance upon its activities. Any sabotage, or any armed rising, was simply to be regarded as a bonus. It is not easy to quantify the achievements of these patriotic men and women, but it is evident that they tied up thousands of enemy soldiers by their very existence. By ambush and sabotage they inflicted serious delays on the German reserves as they moved up to battle during the summer of 1944.

Besides armies that actually existed the Allies made good use of others that did not. It was essential to the success of Overlord that the Germans, who still enjoyed a great numerical advantage in land forces, should be led to make faulty dispositions. It was recognized, of course, that the German commanders were aware of Allied preparations for an assault. At the same time it was thought that, given good security, they might be deceived as to where and

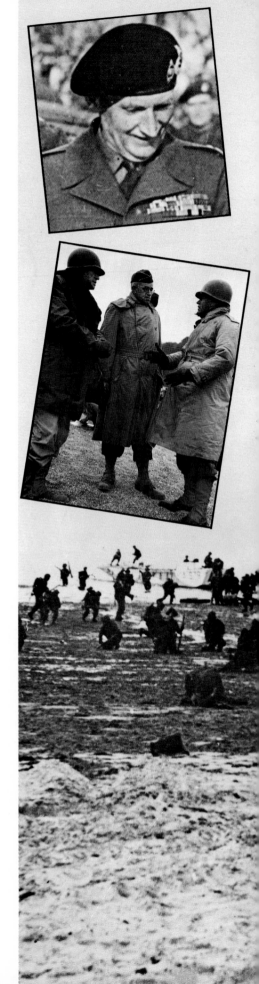

when the landing was to take place. For this reason it was essential that the preliminary bombing did not point to Normandy as the chosen beachhead. Therefore, for every target attacked in the actual assault area, two were bombed elsewhere, especially in the Pas de Calais. This cover plan greatly increased the number of sorties which had to be flown by the Allied air forces, and therefore their casualties, but its strategic success cannot be doubted.

In order to misrepresent their overall strategy the Allies devised a deception plan (code named Bodyguard). This was supplemented by Fortitude which was the cover plan for Normandy. The story that the Allies tried to sell was that the campaign of 1944 would open with the invasion of southern Norway. Then, in about the third week of July, the main

attack would be launched against the Pas de Calais. Dummy landing craft were assembled in southeastern ports and harbors; radio traffic, training exercises and so on built up the desired impression. Even after D-Day the belief was encouraged that the attack on Normandy was a diversionary one.

The fictitious invasion of Norway was entrusted to Lieutenant General Sir A F A N Thorne, Commander in Chief, Northern Command. His 'Fourth Army,' consisting of three imaginary corps, was assembled in Scotland. There were *some* troops in Scotland, but for the most part the Fourth was a phantom army, conjured out of the air by radio traffic from a skeleton headquarters consisting largely of signals staff. Troop movements and exercises, and some well-calculated leaks pointed to landings on

the Norwegian coast. This deception was to be maintained until July. Hitler was sensitive to any threat to Norway. Infuriated by the commando raid which wiped out the garrison of Vaagso on 27 December 1941, he had built up the garrison of Norway to some 300,000 men. It was essential to the Allies that they should not be moved to France, where only 100,000 of them would have added greatly to the defensive power of Army Group West. The Fourth Army was by no means the least effective of the armies that 'fought' on the Allied side in World War II.

The imaginary invasion of the Pas de Calais was scheduled for mid-July. A mythical assault force of 12 divisions was to be built up to 50 divisions. There were, of course, many real formations in east and southeast England. These made themselves

Top left: General Bernard Montgomery commanded all land forces on D-Day.
Far left: Omar Bradley (center) commanded the Americans.
Left and below: Allied troops assemble and train for D-Day.

appear even more formidable than they were by increasing the volume of radio traffic. Nothing was neglected that might add to the desired impression. Inspired leaks through the press, as well as through diplomatic and underground channels built up the picture. In the southeastern counties, forces – real and imaginary – were assembled openly, while in the southwest no effort of concealment was spared. German situation maps showing Allied dispositions in Britain prove the extent to which these deceptions worked.

Their success was helped by the fact that Hitler had been convinced at the outset that the Allies' main assault would come against the Pas de Calais. Indeed all the German leaders were convinced that it should be strongly guarded. This view was not unreasonable. It was the shortest sea route from England to France, and the shortest route for an Allied thrust at the industrial Ruhr. The German leaders thought it probable that the Allies would attack in several places, but opinions differed as to where the subsidiary assaults would land. Norway, the Atlantic coast, Portugal and the Mediterranean coast of France all came under discussion. In October 1943 von Rundstedt pointed out that 'Normandy with Cherbourg, and Brittany with Brest are additional important

Left: A German infantryman mans his defensive position.
Below: A heavy gun pokes from its massive concrete emplacement.
Right: The text of General Eisenhower's message announcing the invasion.
Below right: The Allied commanders, from top left, Bradley, Ramsay, Leigh-Mallory, Bedell-Smith, Tedder, Eisenhower, Montgomery.

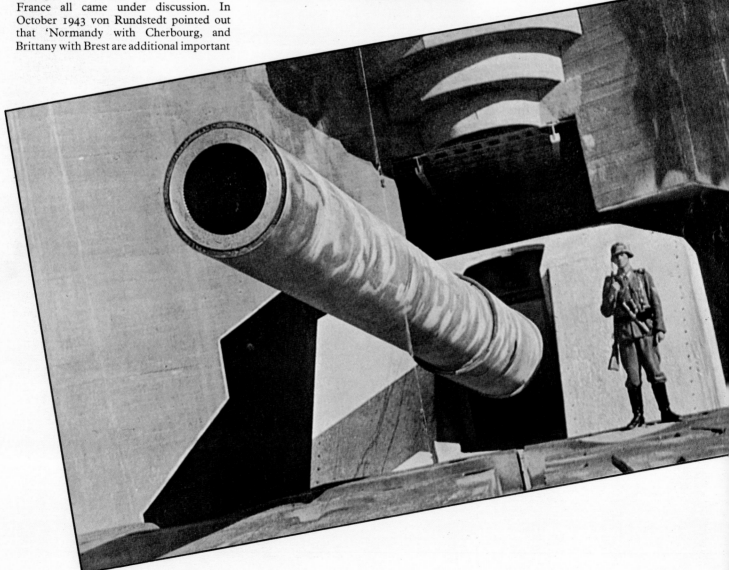

15

THE FOLLOWING IS FOR YOUR INFORMATION AND NOT FOR BROADCAST OR
PUBLICATION
GREEN PRIORITY STAND—BY FOR PRIORITY TRAFFIC   RESUME TRAFFIC

BLUE

WAR V JBJB
FROM JBJB
TO COMBINED CHIEFS OF STAFF WASHINGTON D C
COMMUNIQUE NUMBER ONE IS ABOUT TO BE RELEASED.

RED   URGENT URGENT — JUNE, 6, 1944 9:15 AM

WAR JDJD V JBJB
FROM JBJB

TO OFFICE OF WAR INFORMATION FOREIGN NEWS BUREAU WASHINGTON D.C.

COMMUNIQUE NUMBER ONE SUPREME HEADQUARTERS ALLIED EXPEDITIONARY FORCE

UNDER THE COMMAND OF GENERAL EISENHOWER, ALLIED NAVAL FORCES,

SUPPORTED BY STRONG AIR FORCES, BEGAN LANDING ALLIED ARMIES THIS

MORNING ON THE NORTHERN COAST OF FRANCE.

END COMMUNIQUE

areas on the Channel front,' and, though it took him some time, it seems that Hitler came to think there was something in this. By 4 March 1944 he was describing them as 'particularly threatened' and two days later General Alfred Jodl, his personal Chief of Staff, told von Rundstedt that the Führer attached 'particular importance to Normandy,' and especially Cherbourg. This led to the reinforcement of the Cotentin peninsula by the 91st Airlanding Division, 6th Parachute Regiment and other units. In April the 21st Panzer Division was moved from Brittany to Caen and the Panzer *Lehr* Division from Hungary to Chartres.

Von Rundstedt's forecasts of Allied intentions were pretty sound. In his situation report of 15 May he emphasized the Allies' need to capture big harbors:

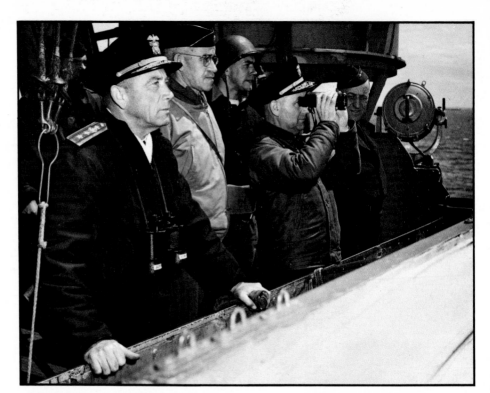

'Le Havre and Cherbourg are primarily to be considered for this purpose, Boulogne and the Cotentin peninsula in the first phase would therefore seem very natural. . . .'

On 29 May he concluded that the air attacks on the Seine bridges 'may indicate enemy designs on Normandy (formation of a bridgehead).'

The Allies, in fact, intended to land three airborne and five seaborne divisions between the River Dives and the Cherbourg Peninsula, and to form a beachhead, which would include the towns of Caen, Bayeux and St Lô. The role of the airborne divisions was to secure the flanks of the beachhead, while the seaborne divisions pushed inland.

On the eve of the invasion there were three German infantry divisions guarding the beaches where the five Allied seaborne divisions were to land. Of these, the 709th and 716th Divisions were static and the 352nd Division was a field division. In support south of Caen was the 21st Panzer Division, a powerful armored formation under Major General Edgar Feuchtinger.

The HQ of the German LXXXIV Corps was near St Lô. It was commanded by General Erich Marcks, a tall, scholarly looking man, who had lost a leg in Russia.

It may be doubted whether the German forces in the area selected for the Allied landing were in themselves sufficient to hurl the invaders into the sea. It cannot be said that either the 709th or 716th Divisions were particularly formidable formations. Much would depend on the handling of the 21st Panzer. Much more would depend on the speed with which these divisions could be reinforced. Some help might be expected fairly soon from the 711st Division, static though it was, and from the 77th Field Division. Although these might help to hold the ring, they were not likely to turn the tide of battle. However, the Germans had three more armored divisions disposed where they might intervene in Normandy. These were the 116th Panzer, just east of the Seine, the 12th SS Panzer and Panzer

Top left: Rear Admiral Alan G Kirk (foreground) commanded the US Western Task Force.

Far left: The battleships USS *Nevada* and USS *Texas* in line astern.

Lehr. Much would depend on the speed with which the Germans could get all, or some, of these into the battle.

In May German air reconnaissance seldom reached even the south coast of England. Nevertheless, on 4 June Admiral Krancke expressed doubts as to 'whether the enemy has yet assembled his invasion fleet in the required strength.' Next day, Army Group B, with no fresh intelligence at hand but noting the concentration of Allied bombing between Dieppe and Dunkirk considered that it pointed to 'the previously assumed focal point of the major landing' (the Pas de Calais). 'As yet,' wrote von Rundstedt that same day, 'there is no immediate prospect of the invasion.' Rommel left his headquarters to stay with his family for a night, on his way to visit Hitler.

So, on the eve of D-Day the Germans were off their guard, the weather was foul in the channel, and the eight Allied divisions were yearning to go. Why should 150,000 or so young men be so keen to stick their necks out? How did they come to be so well motivated? Every unit had been visited by the King or Ike, Monty, Dempsey, Bradley, or various other leaders, who had stressed the importance of the operation which was about to be launched. The British soldier is not lacking in cynicism, and this may well apply to the GI as well. The reason why the men were so eager to get cracking was that in the interests of security they had been assembled in tented camps, surrounded by barbed wire, where they had spent no less than a week. They had been allowed out only in formed groups, and had little to do but watch old films – *Claudia* springs to mind – and listen to a few more pep talks. The terrors of the West Wall were as nothing compared to a few more days in the Allied version of the Concentration Camp.

At 0415 hours on Sunday 4 June the Allied Commanders in Chief were told that the weather forecast for the 5th heralded poor visibility and low cloud over the beaches with rising seas in a mounting gale. Eisenhower had no alternative but to postpone the invasion for 24 hours. The bombarding warships on their way from Scotland had to turn back. The parts of Rear Admiral Kirk's convoy that were already on their way to the Utah assault area had to be recalled. Not until 0900 hours on Sunday 5 June was Admiral Ramsay certain that all units were on their way back to shelter.

At 2130 hours the Commanders in Chief met once more in the library at Southwick House. They were told that a break in the weather was coming. The rain in the assault area was going to clear up for 48 hours. The wind would drop, though the sea would still be rough and choppy. Heavy bombing would be possible on Monday night, 5 June. Another postponement would mean that D-Day would have to be put off for two weeks, with all the ill effects that would bring to the assault troops who were keyed up for action.

Eisenhower asked each senior commander for his opinion. Leigh-Mallory and Tedder thought it would be 'chancy.' Ramsay – whose opinion in such a matter must have held great weight – thought that the assault should go ahead, and Montgomery agreed with him.

Eisenhower reflected for a while, and then made his decision:

'I am quite positive we must give the order. . . . I don't like it, but there it is. . . . I don't see how we can possibly do anything else.'

2. THE AIRBORNE ASSAULT

The airborne assault was a vital part of Operation Overlord. The Allies sent in three airborne divisions (see appendix for breakdown), two American and one British, to prepare for the main assault by taking certain strategic points and by disrupting German communications.

The task of the British 6th Airborne Division was to hold the eastern flank of the beachhead. This called for the seizure of the bridges over the River Orne, between Caen and the sea, and the capture of the Merville battery, which could enfilade the lodgment area, posing a dangerous threat to the left flank of the seaborne landings. In general it was intended to deny the Germans the rather rough tract of wooded and flooded country between the rivers Orne and Dives. It was a tall order for a single division, even though it was to be reinforced by 1st Commando Brigade, which was to land from the sea.

Experience, especially in Sicily, had shown that landing parachutists and gliders on a windy night is a hazardous business. A large proportion of the troops engaged are certain to be dropped in the wrong place. Commanders who find themselves in the right place too often find themselves with no more than a handful of the troops allotted to their task. Lest this should seem too gloomy a picture it must be appreciated that the enemy commander, studying his map and marking every report of a hostile landing, will be doubly confused if some of the attackers have landed in the wrong place. The problem of where and when to launch the defenders' reserves – and there are never enough of these – becomes more intractable. So if some pilots lose their way, and if others release their gliders at the first burst of flak, some good may still come of it so long as the airborne troops do *something* on landing. The men of the 6th Airborne Division, as the Germans soon learned, would make a nuisance of themselves wherever they landed!

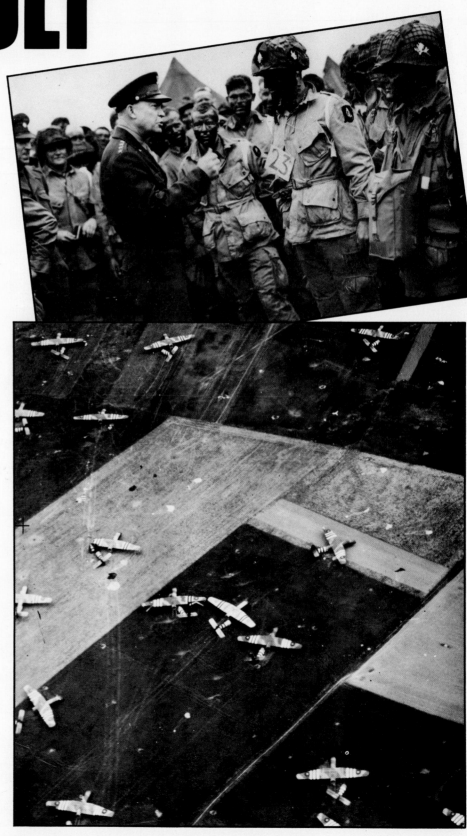

Top right: Eisenhower talks with paratroops before D-Day.
Right: British Horsa gliders on their landing zone near Caen.
Opposite: American gliders landed on the Cherbourg Peninsula, west of the main seaborne landings.

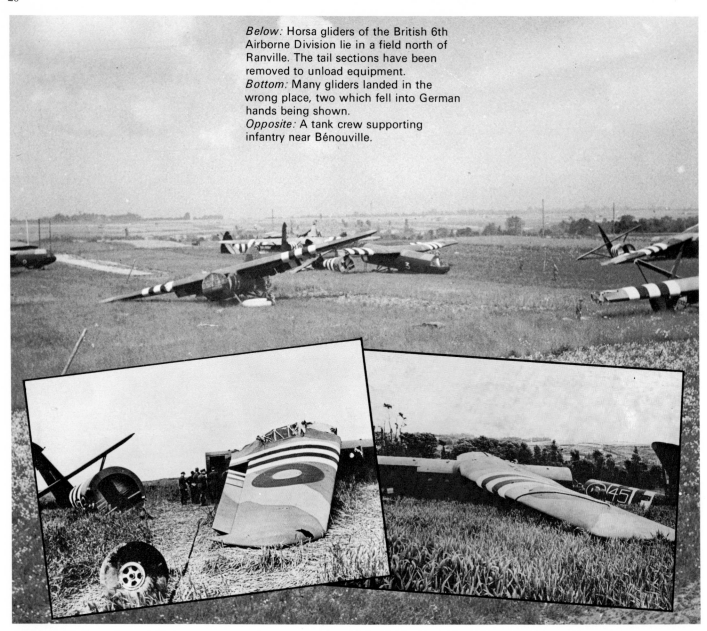

Major R J Howard was charged with the surprise capture of the Bénouville and Ranville bridges. His party comprised five platoons of the 2nd Oxfordshire and Buckinghamshire Light Infantry and 30 officers and men of the 249th Field Company, Royal Engineers. They crossed the French coast just after midnight, and six Horsa gliders were released. The first stuck its nose into the German wire surrounding the Bénouville bridge, and two others touched down within 100 yards. Two of the other gliders landed within 150 yards of the Ranville bridge. Both bridges were rushed and within 15 minutes had been taken, intact. Casualties were light, though the leading platoon commander was killed. The sappers found that the bridges had not been prepared for demolition. German prisoners from the 736th Grenadier Regiment of the 716th Infantry Division were taken.

To have taken the bridges was a great exploit, but unless they could be held there would be no communication with the troops who landed east of the Orne. Howard took up a defensive position about the bridges. There was a good deal of desultory firing for there were German troops in the nearby villages of Bénouville and Ranville. A troop of three tanks approached, but was discouraged when the leader was hit by a PIAT (Projector Infantry Anti-Tank). The PIAT weighed 34.5 pounds and was a short-range weapon. It hurled a 2.5-pound bomb and was supposed to be effective at 100 yards, but it is thought that its successes were, generally speaking, scored at point-blank range.

A little later the German officer in command of the bridge defenses drove up in his car and was captured. This classic *coup de main* had been pulled off without one of the six gliders, which, released too far east, had landed eight miles from the target.

The task of 3rd Parachute Brigade was to cut the bridges over the River Dives, so as to delay German troops advancing to attack the British left flank. It was to occupy the high ground commanding these approaches, and to capture the Merville battery. The task of the 5th Parachute Brigade was to capture and hold the Orne crossings.

Every operation of war, however successful, has its share of *friction de guerre* (grit in the works). A typical example of this complicated operations for the 3rd Brigade. A path-finder party which was to land on dropping zone K was dropped in error on zone N where, in all innocence, it began to send out the code letter K and to call in more troops of the 3rd Brigade. It was some time before this mistake could be put right.

The 5th Brigade was carried in 129 aircraft. All but five dropped their troops, but they were greatly dispersed and much time was lost while searching for equipment containers in the dark, and while trying to find the rendezvous.

It was 0130 hours before half the 7th Battalion and 591st Parachute Squadron, Royal Engineers, found their way to the rendezvous, without many of their machine guns, mortars and radios. They were sent to reinforce Major Howard. There was confused fighting in the villages of Bénouville and le Port, and the Germans actually overran the Regimental Aid Post, killing the chaplain! When dawn came the fighting was still going on, but the vital bridges were still in British hands.

The task of 12th Battalion was to hold the eastern approaches to the Ranville bridge. Fifteen of its 32 aircraft dropped their passengers accurately. Seven others were less than a mile out. The other 10 were wildly adrift. By 0400 hours the Battalion had occupied Le Bas de Ranville and taken prisoners from 736th Grena-

dier Regiment.

Meanwhile 13th Battalion, whose task was to take Ranville and, with some sapper units, to clear and improve Drop Zone N, had taken its objective. They had also captured some men of 125th Panzer Grenadier Regiment, which belonged to 21st Panzer Division, stationed southeast of Caen.

At about 0330 hours the 68 Horsas of the third flight crossed the coast. Fifty – 25 of them somewhat damaged by flak – landed with few casualties. Low cloud now obscured the coast and some of the 18 missing gliders were simply lost. In other cases, no doubt, the towropes had parted. This wave brought in nine 6-pounder and two 17-pounder antitank guns, heavy engineer stores and equipment, and Major General Richard Nelson Gale. One may imagine his relief when he learned that the *coup de main* had been successful, and that the bridgehead was holding out.

Meanwhile 3rd Brigade, though widely dispersed, had been carrying out a variety of tasks. The commander of 8th Battalion, with 160 men who had landed correctly on zone K, had taken up a position on the high ground southwest of the Bois de Bavent, so as to cover a party which was demolishing the Bures bridge. Troops that had landed by mistake in Zone N also made for the high ground west of the Bois de Bavent. Most of 3rd Parachute Squadron was sent to blow the Bures bridge, but Major J C A Roseveare, with an officer and seven sappers crowded into a jeep and trailer full of explosives and made for Troarn. At the entrance to the village they ran into a barbed-wire knife-rest. In the dark it took them 20 minutes to clear this obstacle out of the way. They sent out a scout, who shot a German cyclist. The garrison stood to arms. The jeep dashed through the village with 'a Boche in every doorway shooting like mad.' Firing back, they hurtled down the slope to the river and, astonishingly, they only lost one man on their reckless ride. Working as fast as they could they blew a wide gap in the center span of the bridge. Abandoning the jeep they made their way across country and rejoined their party, who had blown the Bures bridge, swimming several small streams on the way.

The Canadian Battalion had a stiff fight at Varaville and captured the château there, though a pillbox held out. A valiant Frenchman, putting on a red beret, armed himself with a rifle and is credited with slaying three snipers in the nearby woods. Here, as at Amfreville and the other villages of

this area, the civilians came out to tend the wounded.

By far the worst task that fell to 3rd Brigade was the destruction of the Merville battery. It was thought that it had four guns. If it was not destroyed before daylight it would command the beaches on which 3rd Infantry Division and 1st Commando Brigade were to land. L F Ellis in Volume I of *Victory in the West* describes the position:

'The guns were in steel-doored concrete emplacements six feet thick, two of which were also covered by twelve feet of earth. They were in a fenced area of seven hundred

by five hundred yards within which was a belt of barbed wire, double in places, fifteen feet thick and five feet high. An anti-tank ditch was incomplete but mines had been sown profusely and there were a dual-purpose gun position and about fifteen weapon pits. Outside the main position was a wired in strong-point with five machine-gun emplacements and several other anti-aircraft gun positions.'

(It so happens that the author was in this position two days later. Believe me it was a stinker.) The task of destroying the position fell to Lieutenant Colonel Terence Otway

Utah — PLANNED AIRBORNE DROPPING AND LANDING ZONES

Utah — ASSAULT AREAS

→ FIRST ASSAULT WAVES

⇠ ATTACKS BY BRITISH 6 AIRBORNE DIVISION

◯ HELD BY ALLIES AT 2400 HRS ON D-DAY

⋯ ALLIED OBJECTIVE AT 2400 HRS ON D-DAY

RCT — US REGIMENTAL COMBAT TEAM

709 Inf Div — SITUATION OF GERMAN UNITS AT DAWN ON D-DAY

▨ HELD BY GERMAN TROOPS AT 2400 HRS ON D-DAY

➤ COUNTERATTACKS BY 21 PANZER DIVISION

⫴ MAJOR GERMAN GUN BATTERIES

≣ FLOODED AREAS (PRAIRIES MARÉCAGEUSES)

+ GLIDER LANDINGS

MILES 0 ... 10

KILOMETERS 0 ... 10 ... 15

and the 9th Parachute Battalion. It would have been difficult enough had the whole operation gone according to plan. The intention was to use a small reconnaissance party and three companies. One, which was to be a firm base on which to rally, was to make a diversion against the main entrance. A second was to breach the defenses. A third was to make the assault. As a sort of bonus a party, carried in three gliders, was to crash land on the battery just as the assault went in. All this was to be accomplished in four and a half hours of darkness. It was not an easy task.

The reconnaissance party dropped as planned and set off for the battery. That was just about all that *did* go according to plan. Much equipment was lost in the flooded area round Varaville, and only half the Battalion dropped within a mile of the rendezvous. At 0255 hours Otway set off with 150 men. He arrived to find that his reconnaissance party had done rather well They had cut the outer wire, marked paths through the minefield *with their feet*, and dealt with a number of booby traps.

Otway reorganized his men into seven parties. Two were to breach the main wire, four were to deal with the four guns and one was to make a diversion at the main entrance. At this juncture two of the Albemarles appeared, and flew around looking for the place to crash land. It had not been possible to put out lights to guide them, but eventually the gliders were released, landing 200 yards away. Their troops engaged the Germans in the perimeter defenses.

Otway's seven parties went into action; the wire was breached and the main gate stormed. The garrison was overwhelmed in a brief and bloody assault. The 75mm guns were put out of action. Then the Battalion's signal officer took 'a somewhat ruffled pigeon' from his pocket and sent it off to England to report the success. The bird was probably glad to leave.

This assault cost Otway's party 70 casualties. With the 80 survivors he made for his next objective, the high ground at Le Plein. In German hands this would have given their gunners wonderful observation posts, overlooking 3rd Infantry Division's area.

So, when dawn came 6th Airborne Division could claim that, despite every sort of accident, it had carried out all its main tasks. The Orne bridges were held. Three of the bridges over the Dives – Troarn, Bures, and Robehomme – had been blown, as well as another over a tributary at Varaville. The Merville battery was out of action. The beginnings of a defensive position was being formed on the high ground that runs from Le Plein to Troarn; vital ground. If the Germans could reconquer the area between Dives and the Orne they could render the beachhead untenable, and drive the Allies back into the sea.

At 0840 hours the 1st Commando Brigade under Brigadier Lord Lovat, DSO, MC, began to land west of Ouistreham. By midday the leading commando, 6, had reached the Bénouville bridge. It was deployed to strengthen the line on the high ground at Le Plein. This brigade, some 2000 strong, consisted of 3, 4, 6 and 45 (Royal Marine) Commandos.

Meanwhile two American Airborne Divisions, 82nd and 101st, had been dropped all over the Cotentin peninsula. Their task was to aid the assault of the United States First Army and facilitate the capture of the vital Cotentin peninsula. It was an ambitious plan. Some 18,000 men were to be dropped by night into an area of Normandy bocage and floods. The German defenders were more numerous than in the tract of country between the Orne and the Dives. The German troops were mostly from 91st Division. This unit had been specially trained to combat airborne attacks.

In order to avoid the antiaircraft defenses of Cherbourg the American IX Troop Carrier Command made an indirect approach via the Channel Islands. They were protected by Mosquitos of Air Defence of Great Britain, while Stirlings of Bomber Command dropped 'window' so as to deceive the German radar. The bombers went on further south to simulate diversionary landings.

As soon as the airborne forces turned east and crossed the coast of the Cotentin peninsula they ran into heavy flak and small-arms fire. There was thick cloud and formations tended to break up; even the pathfinders found it difficult to identify their targets. In consequence the drops were widely scattered. In *Cross-Channel Attack* G A Harrison describes the scene:

'The first actions of all airborne units in the Cotentin on D-Day were attempts by

Left and right: Groups of paratroops, who had been dropped wide of their assigned landing zones, soon fell into German hands.
Below left: Two privates of the US 101st Airborne Division don Indian warpaint before their drop.
Below: An American reconnaissance aircraft took this photograph of Horsa and Hadrian gliders within hours of their landing.

small groups of men to carry out in the fog of the battlefield their own portion of the assigned plan. There could be little overall direction from above.'

The accounts of what they achieved, especially those of 101st Airborne, are thin indeed. *Time* magazine supplements the official records. An officer told of seeing German tracer ripping through men's parachutes as they descended. In *D-Day* Warren Tute relates that:

'In one plane, a soldier laden with his 90 pounds of equipment got momentarily stuck in the door. A 20mm shell hit him in the belly. Fuse-caps in his pockets began to go off. Part of the wounded man's load was TNT. Before this human bomb could explode, his mates behind him pushed him out. The last they saw of him, his parachute had opened and he was drifting to earth in a shroud of bursting flame.'

General Matthew B Ridgway, the commander of 82nd Airborne Division, parachuted to earth and, collecting 11 officers and men, set up his HQ in an orchard. He wrote:

'The Germans were all around us, of course, sometimes within 500 yards of my command post, but in the fierce and confused fighting that was going on all about they did not launch the strong attack that could have wiped out our eggshell perimeter defenses.'

The 82nd Airborne was meant to be dropped astride the Merderet, to capture Ste Mère Eglise and to facilitate the advance into the Cotentin. Only one regiment was dropped at all accurately and in a brilliant action a party from this unit quickly seized and held the village. The other troops of the division were scattered up to 25 miles away; many were left struggling in the marshy ground on either side of the Merderet.

The 101st Division was also widely dispersed but senior officers were able to collect parties and move toward the causeways inland from Utah which were their main objectives. Other groups managed to take bridgeheads over the Douve which would later be important in allowing a link with the Omaha forces. Although at dawn perhaps only 1000 of the division's men were under command they did manage to give valuable aid to the forces moving inland from Utah.

Chaos reigned in the Cotentin that night. Everywhere the paratroops – their efforts supplemented by French saboteurs – were cutting the telephone lines. Even so news of the first landings got through to LXXXIV Corps HQ at St Lô:

'At 0111 hours – unforgettable moment – the field telephone rang. Something important was coming through; while listen-

Below: The crew of an RAF Bomber Command Short Stirling bomber pose with their aircraft. Stirlings were also used as transports and glider tugs by the airborne forces.

ing to it, the General [Marcks] stood up stiffly, his hand gripping the edge of the table. With a nod, he beckoned his Chief of Staff to listen in. "Enemy parachute troops dropped east of the Orne estuary. Main area Breville–Ranville and the north edge of the Bavent Forest. Countermeasures are in progress." '

This message, which came from 716th Division (Lieutenant General W Richter) galvanized Marcks' HQ. 'The Corps Command post resembled a disturbed beehive,' wrote one of its staff officers, 'Priority messages were sent in all directions.' Marcks, in no doubt that this was the invasion, sent out the signal 'Alarm coast,' and between 0111 hours and dawn the warning went by field telephones to his units and formations. The information was passed to OKW (Armed Forces High Command) and to von Rundstedt's GHQ.

At OKW Field Marshal Wilhelm Keitel thought that the landing in Normandy must be a diversion. The real invasion would come at Calais. He was not going to wake the Führer for a false alarm. A better general than he, von Rundstedt, also believed this was a diversion and that the real blow was still to come – in the Pas de Calais.

In the prevailing confusion it was not strange that some of the generals on both sides simply did not know what was going on. Falley of the 91st Airborne Division went to find out for himself and was ambushed by American paratroops. This was reported to Ridgway whose comment was:

'Well, in our present situation, killing Divisional Commanders does not strike me as being particularly hilarious.'

Below left: Dead American soldiers await burial at Ste Mère Eglise. Total Allied casualties by the end of August were 209,672.
Bottom: Allied troops mopping up at Breville after a night assault against the village on 12 June.
Below: German dead collected for burial at Ste Mère Eglise on 7 June were among the 80,783 casualties suffered by Army Group B that month.

3. BREACHING THE ATLANTIC WALL

As the assault fleet butted its way through the gale in the Channel, and the airborne divisions flew into France, the heavy bombers of Bomber Command set off to attack the 10 most dangerous coast-defense batteries. Three of them had to be attacked early on, for Allied airborne troops would be landing near them soon after midnight. These were the Merville battery and those at Fontenay and St Martin de Varreville in the Cotentin. The other seven were to be bombed between 0315–0500 hours, so that they would scarcely have time to recover before dawn, when the naval bombardment would begin. These were the batteries at La Pernelle, Maisy, Pointe du Hoe, Longues, Mont Fleury, Ouistreham and Houlgate.

On average each battery received 500 tons of bombs delivered by about 100 aircraft. Of 1056 Lancaster, Halifax and Mosquito aircraft 11 did not return and 70 crew were lost.

Right: The British battleship HMS *Rodney* bombards the German defenses near Caen. Her main armament comprised nine 16-inch guns, supplemented by 12 6-inch guns.

Above: Armorers of the USAAF Eighth
Air Force with 0.5-inch machine guns
and belts of ammunition in front of a
North American P-51D Mustang fighter.
Right: Boeing B-17 Flying Fortresses
fly in formation over England.

32

Right: The bridge over the Seine at Mantes was badly damaged by Allied bombers in a campaign aimed at isolating the invasion beachhead from reinforcements.
Far right: French refugees hastily evacuated the invasion area to escape Allied bombardment.
Below: Supermarine Spitfires were used to spot the fall of naval shells. This aircraft was flown by US Navy Squadron VCS-7.

Meanwhile in the ships and landing craft the invaders were spending a truly horrible night, thrown about by the violence of the gale, and for the most part seasick. As their craft pitched and rolled veterans of Sicily took what comfort they could from the thought that rough weather tended to put the Germans off their guard. Indeed, both at sea and in the air the Germans remained totally inactive. No aircraft seems to have spotted the assault fleet streaming into the Channel as darkness fell. No watcher on the coast of Normandy seems to have observed the Allied minesweepers at work.

Meanwhile two bomber squadrons, fitted with radar-jamming equipment, were masking the Germans' warning system. To add to the confusion dummy airborne landings were being made at Mattot, Marigny and Yvetot, the last being intended to suggest that an attack north of the Seine was planned. Feints by motor launches and aircraft were made near Boulogne and in the Dieppe and le Havre area, but there seems to have been little enemy reaction.

Soon after 0500 hours the British bombarding squadrons, guided in by the midget submarines *X20* and *X23* which were flashing green lights to seaward, began to take up their positions, and at about 0530 hours the fleet opened fire. Fifty miles of the Normandy coast rocked as salvo after salvo of heavy shells tore into the fortifications of the West Wall, and as ton after ton of bombs hailed down from the sky. One can imagine the Germans, many of them alerted soon after midnight by messages from LXXXIV Corps, peering through the loopholes of their fortifications and trying, despite smoke and debris, to make out the ships and craft bearing down upon the beaches.

The bombardment fell upon the German defenders and the French inhabitants alike. The French, for the most part, stayed in their homes, even when these overlooked the beaches. At Ver sur Mer an elderly

couple was found dead in bed, without a scratch on either of them. On 6 June 1944 an enormous weight of bombs and shells was delivered in the space of a few hours. It was a crucial phase of the operation and, of course, a tremendous encouragement to the men in the landing craft as they ran in, head-on, to sample whatever the West Wall might have in store for them.

With the dawn, wave after wave of day fighters began to come over, spreading out across the whole battlefield, ready to engage enemy aircraft or army reinforcements. A ceaseless patrol by four squadrons of Lightnings was kept up over the mine-free lanes which had been swept across the Channel. Thirty-six squadrons of Spitfires ensured that there were always six squadrons giving low cover over the assault area. Above the clouds, at about 8000 feet, three out of 16 squadrons of American Thunderbolts maintained a constant patrol. There were 30 reserve squadrons, which had six ready at all times as an immediate striking force. This mass of aircraft flew overhead unchallenged. Not a single German plane intervened during the first hours of the invasion. There were Dunkirk veterans in the invasion force – not very many perhaps, but some. To them the air situation was a pleasant change.

Under this unparalleled air cover the warships came in to bombard. On the exposed eastern flank HMS *Warspite*, *Ramillies* and *Roberts* opened fire, at about 0530 hours, with their 15-inch guns upon the batteries east of the Orne, at Villerville, Bénerville and Houlgate. It was an unforgettable sight. Battleships, cruisers, destroyers and support landing craft were engaging targets all along the British front. Admiral Krancke complained in his war diary that 'it was only to be expected that no effective blow could be struck at such a superior enemy force,' but in fact the German Navy did strike back. Allied aircraft had laid a smoke screen to shield

the anchorage from the heavy batteries at Le Havre. Three enterprising German torpedo boats dashed through the screen and sank the Norwegian warship *Svenner* before disappearing into the smoke. This startling attack was the only maritime riposte the enemy made that morning.

For the most part the fire of the German Coast Defense batteries was desultory and ineffective. However, the four-gun battery at Longues, though engaged by *Ajax* at 0530 hours, opened up on the headquarters ship, *Bulolo*, at about 0600 hours. It was silenced by 0620 but it reopened fire later and compelled *Bulolo* to move seaward. The cruisers *Ajax* and *Argonaut* then took on the battery. It received 179 shells, and two of its guns were put out of action by direct hits through the embrasures. By 0845 hours the battery was silenced. The Bénerville battery, though silenced at the outset by *Ramillies*, opened up later and compelled *Warspite* to move her berth. To their credit it must be said that there were some determined German fighters at Longues and Bénerville.

By this time a fantastic regatta had begun. All along the front the assault craft were manned and lowered into the choppy sea for the final run in. In the American sector 269 medium bombers, Marauders of the Ninth Air Force, flew over to blast the defenses of Utah and silenced most of them. Bad visibility over the other beaches precluded pinpoint visual attacks on batteries and strong points. Instead wave after wave of aircraft flew in, in line abreast, releasing their bombs on the orders of pathfinders aiming by instruments.

About five minutes before H-hour some 38,000 five-inch explosive rockets deluged the beaches. They were fired electrically from assault craft, each of which was capable of launching 1000 rockets in 90 seconds. As their salvoes finished exploding the first seaborne soldiers of the invading armies set foot on shore.

4. OMAHA AND UTAH

The American landings were made on Utah and Omaha. Utah proved to be the easiest landing, and Omaha the most difficult of the whole Allied assault. The Utah beaches, on the east coast of the Cotentin, were assailed by VII Corps under Lieutenant General J L Collins. The Omaha beaches, between Vire and Port en Bessin were attacked by V Corps under Lieutenant General L T Gerow.

The Americans had decided to go in at 0630 hours, about an hour earlier than the British owing to the difference in tides. At low tide it would be easier to clear the obstacles. The naval bombardment was not to open until 0550, 20 minutes later than on the British front. The defenses on the beaches where the British landed suffered two hours bombardment before H-Hour, as opposed to only 40 minutes on the American front. With the benefit of hindsight Admiral Kirk, commanding the Western Task Force commented that:

'the period of bombardment was extremely heavy but was of too short duration to silence or neutralize all the defenses, particularly in the Omaha area.'

Rear Admiral Hall was of the same opinion:

'the time available for the prelanding bombardment was not sufficient for the destruction of beach defense targets.'

Another major difference between the American and British plans was the choice of the lowering positions ('transport areas'), where the troops transferred from ships into landing craft. The American lowering position was 11 miles from the coast, the British only seven. The American soldiers running in to Utah and Omaha had to put

Below: US infantrymen wade ashore from their landing craft, which has grounded on Utah Beach.
Below right: Survivors from a landing craft sunk off Utah Beach are helped ashore.

up with three hours in small craft in rougher conditions than any they had met with during training. For those approaching Utah this was not so bad for their run in was sheltered under the lee of the Cotentin peninsula. Force U had one piece of bad luck. It ran into an undetected minefield, and lost the navigational leader of the left-hand assault group, which had four DD (amphibious) tanks aboard, and the destroyer *Corry*.

The US 4th Infantry Division made the opening attacks on Utah. By mistake the landings all took place on the southern part of the beach which happened to be less well defended. The landing began punctually at 0630 hours against slight opposition, which was quickly overcome. The 28 DD tanks still available swam in 3000 yards and landed safely some minutes behind the infantry. The engineers and naval demolition parties set to work to destroy the beach obstacles, and cleared them within an hour, giving landing craft a clear run in. This was an achievement which could not be paralleled anywhere else on the whole front.

Above: The forward 14-inch guns of USS *Nevada* in action.
Left: Minesweepers clearing the approaches to Utah.

Above: A German soldier lies dead before the pillbox that he defended on Utah Beach. Preliminary bombardment left these defenses largely undamaged.
Above right: By the evening of D-day the beaches had become crowded with men and equipment.
Right: Wounded American troops are evacuated from the beaches by an LCM (Landing Craft, Mechanized).

The infantry now pushed inland with the object of capturing the causeway roads leading to Pouppeville, Ste Marie du Mont and Audouville la Hubert. Meanwhile, follow-up troops, vehicles and equipment were coming in unopposed, their movement inland was delayed only by the lack of beach exits and the need to breach the sea wall separating the land from the shore.

The first contact between American seaborne and airborne troops took place near Pouppeville, which was attacked at about 0800 hours by a small party of parachutists. Some of the garrison held out until noon.

By 1000 hours there were six battalions ashore and progress inland was delayed by flooding rather than German opposition. This is not to say that there was no resistance. Still, by a combination of accidents some of the leading assault craft missed the stronger German defenses. The mining of the vessel guiding them in and the strong current sweeping down the shoreline brought them in several miles south of of their planned landing place. Brigadier General Theodore Roosevelt Jr, a veteran aged 57 who had persuaded his Divisional Commander to let him go ashore 'to steady the boys,' took the vital decision to push inland, deepening the beachhead for the follow-up troops. Ably supported by Commodore James Arnold, the naval officer in charge of the beachhead, he solved the traffic problem, bringing in

Above: Men of the 101st Airborne Division – the 'Screaming Eagles' – fraternize with French villagers.
Above right: Captured German troops are led down to the beaches.
Above far right: A patrol of paratroopers advances cautiously by the church at St Marcouf.
Right: Advancing troops of the US 4th Infantry Division leave the cover of their trench.
Far right: A German remotely controlled miniature tank is disarmed by a US Navy expert.

troops on Green beach, instead of getting them massacred on Red. It took the Germans three hours to shift their fire and by that time men of the 4th Division were pushing toward Ste Mère Eglise, where the strongest concentration of the 82nd Airborne Division was centered. Force U had landed about 23,250 men with 1742 vehicles and 1695 tons of stores. Although there was room for the buildup at Utah to proceed, the American VII Corps had not yet crossed the River Merderet to the west or pushed southward to join hands with the V Corps at Omaha. There was still a strong German group between Turqueville and Fauville, and a battle group from their 91st Infantry Division, trying to push down the Cherbourg–Carentan road to Ste Mère Eglise, was meeting with stubborn resistance from a small detachment of 82nd Airborne Division at Neuville au Plain.

The 101st Airborne Division was having a difficult time. Of 32 gliders bringing reinforcements, 11 landed in or near Hiesville as planned, but many crashed or fell into the hands of the Germans. Although detachments covered the bridges at La Barquette and near Brévands, between the sea and Carentan, two battalions of the German 6th Parachute Division, counter-attacking from that town, had infiltrated between them and the rest of the 101st Division.

The landing craft plowing toward Omaha were buffeted by a stronger wind and rougher seas than Force U had encountered off Utah. The land behind the sand dunes at Utah is only a few feet above sea level, but the Omaha beaches are overlooked by bluffs which rise in places to 150 feet and command the beaches. Whereas the Utah defenses had been well and truly battered from air and sea, those at Omaha had been missed by the bombers. They were protected from seaward and the 40-minute naval bombardment had been unable to silence the guns. To make matters worse the German troops at Omaha, the 352nd Infantry Division, were not only more numerous than those of the static 709th Division defending Utah, they were also

better soldiers. Moreover, their defensive position, naturally strong, had been skill-fully fortified. There were eight big guns in concrete bunkers, 35 antitank guns in pillboxes, and 85 machine guns, sited to cover three rows of obstacles on the beach below the high-water mark. The four exits from the beach and a belt of shingle, in itself a tank obstacle, had been made more difficult to cross by mines and wire. Within a mile to the rear lay three strong-points, the fortified villages of Colleville sur Mer, St Laurent sur Mer and Vierville sur Mer, giving depth to the position. Beyond them was the flooded valley of the River Aure.

The 12-mile run in to Omaha began in darkness and there was no little confusion in the transport area. Landing craft straggled before they crossed the line of departure. Two, carrying artillery, had actually found-ered before reaching the transport areas. Of the 32 DD tanks, launched 6000 yards offshore, 27 foundered in the rough seas. Landing craft carried 51 to the shore, but

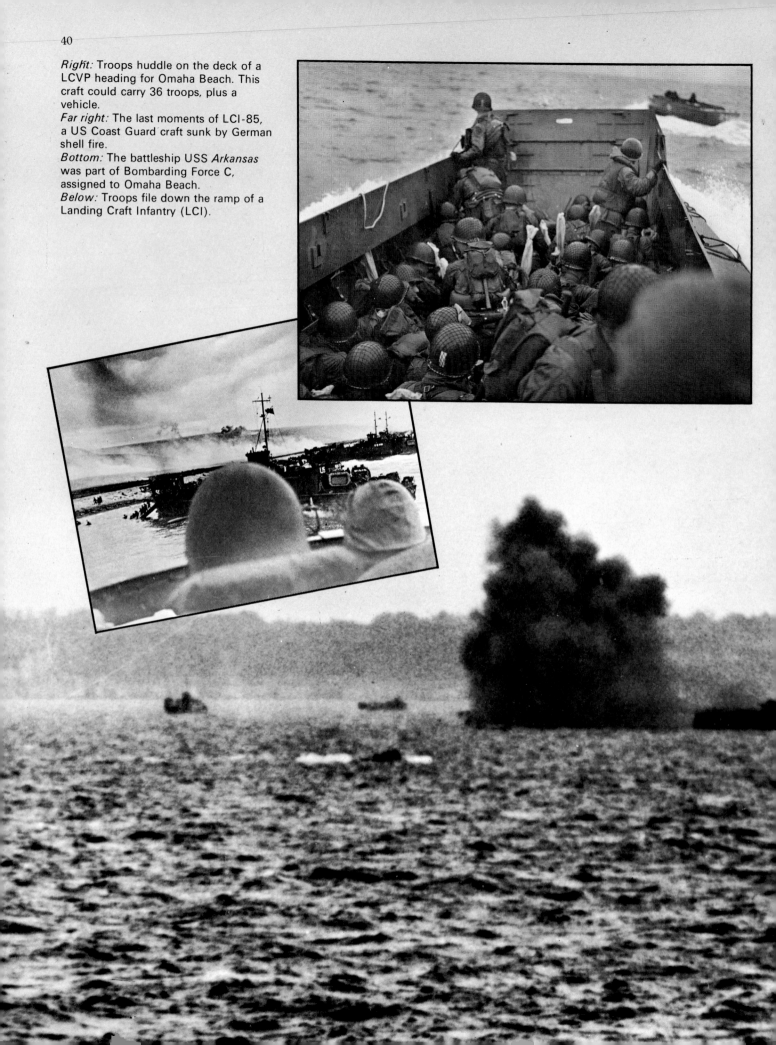

Right: Troops huddle on the deck of a LCVP heading for Omaha Beach. This craft could carry 36 troops, plus a vehicle.

Far right: The last moments of LCI-85, a US Coast Guard craft sunk by German shell fire.

Bottom: The battleship USS *Arkansas* was part of Bombarding Force C, assigned to Omaha Beach.

Below: Troops file down the ramp of a Landing Craft Infantry (LCI).

eight of these were knocked out by gunfire. Not less than 10 of the craft carrying infantry were swamped on the run in, and 22 howitzers and an infantry cannon company were lost. The weather was too much for the DUKWs (amphibious trucks), which carried them, and so the infantry struggled ashore without most of the artillery which was supposed to support it, and without tanks.

The Germans held their fire as the assault craft came in. As soon as the first reached the shore, the defenders opened up with a tremendous fire of guns, mortars and machine guns. A landing craft carrying 35 men was hit by four mortar bombs and simply vanished. Men from another craft, which foundered 1000 yards offshore, were dragged down by the weight of their equipment. The scattered troops, wading ashore, not always with the units to which they belonged, ran into a hail of bullets and sought such cover as they could find. Some tried to conceal themselves behind the German beach obstacles. Others lay in the water and crept in with the rising tide. Nine companies went into the assault. Two bunched in front of Les Moulins, and elements of four got ashore in the Colleville sector. One company was carried far to the east and landed an hour and a half late. The demolition teams had particularly

Left: The bow gunner of a beached LCI engages the German defenses with his 20mm cannon, while the infantry wade ashore.

Bottom right: The American flag marks the position of a command post to prevent it being shelled by friendly forces.

Below: Once the defenses had been overrun, the beachheads became scenes of orderly activity by supporting troops.

heavy casualties, much of their equipment was lost and soon the rising tide rendered their work of beach clearance impossible. Only three out of the 16 bulldozers allotted to the 116th Infantry got ashore, and one of these was hampered in its movements by infantry taking cover behind it!

It was not easy for the American observers to make out where their leading troops had got to. The shells of the battleship *Nevada* had shrouded the scene in a cloud of dust!

The follow-up waves came in to find the survivors of the first wave lying at the water's edge or taking cover under the bank of shingle inland of the beach, or at the foot of the bluff. The German fire had not abated. Admiral Hall describes how:

'wave after wave was dispatched from the line of departure close in on the preceding wave, where the combined effect of the wind and tide soon converted the waves into a milling mass in which little semblance of

order remained. Had it not been for the appearance on the scene of the Deputy Assault Group Commanders and their prompt action in withdrawing and reforming these craft, the success of the entire landing would have been jeopardized.'

It is hardly surprising that the German officer commanding the fortifications at Pointe et Raz de la Percée thought that 'the invasion had been stopped on the beaches.' He could see 10 tanks and a

great many other vehicles burning. The defensive fire of his men had been excellent. He could see the dead and wounded lying in the sand. Even so, at about 0730 hours little parties of determined men had begun to struggle through the barbed wire and were working their way inland through the minefields. Eight United States and three British destroyers gave invaluable fire support at this dangerous period. The tide of battle was turning.

By 0900 hours small groups of American soldiers, which had infiltrated the German posts along the crest, were gradually wiping them out and making their way toward St Laurent and Vierville. Units from 29th and 1st Divisions gathered by Colleville, and with covering fire from a destroyer, had made a gap in the wire and were storming an enemy strongpoint. They had got going again because the officers and non-commissioned officers knew that 'leadership is done from in front.' One, who is deservedly remembered, was Colonel Can-

ham, 'They're murdering us here,' he said to men cowering on the beach, 'Let's move inland and get murdered.'

At about 1000 hours Major General C R Huebner, the assault commander, intervened decisively. He held back the waves of vehicles, whose arrival on the beaches could only add to the confusion, and sent in more combat troops. In response to his call for naval gunfire support, destroyers ran in to within 1000 yards of the shore.

A battalion of the 1st Division, veterans of Sicily and Salerno, fought their way through the minefields to attack Colleville. The 29th Division, which was having a very rough time, infiltrated as far as Vierville and St Laurent. About noon the German gunners began to run out of ammunition and, because of the Allied command of the air, convoys could not get through to replenish it.

Meanwhile three companies of US Rangers were carrying out a bold and unusual exploit against the battery at

Pointe du Hoe. They scaled the cliffs with ropes and ladders and, with covering fire from two destroyers, Satterlee (US) and Talybont (British), stormed the position only to find that the guns had been removed and concealed inland.

There was a time during that morning when a determined counterattack might have driven US V Corps into the sea. In view of the 352nd Division's optimistic reports, General Marcks sent his reserves elsewhere. By nightfall the Americans had possession of a patch of French soil some six miles long, and in places two miles deep. Reinforcements came in during the night until, with over 34,000 men ashore, the beachhead was secure.

The day's fighting had cost V Corps 3000 casualties, 50 tanks, and 26 guns. In addition 50 landing craft and 10 larger vessels were lost.

The plan for the Omaha landing left much to be desired. However, it was the infantrymen who, despite their top brass, fought and won this vital foothold.

Above left: A victim of the first assault wave, a US infantryman, lies dead beside a beach obstacle.
Above far left: Wounded troops of the US 1st Infantry Division find shelter.
Below: Landing Ships Tank (LST) discharge supplies onto Omaha Beach.

5. THE BRITISH LANDINGS

The British Sector was divided into three assault areas and 10 landing beaches, but the troops went in over only five of them. There were five Assault Brigades, or rather brigade groups, an intermediate brigade, and four follow-up brigades. In addition there was 1st SS Brigade (Commandos) and 4th SS Brigade (less 46 [RM] Commando).

The 1st Commando Brigade went in on Queen Beach, with the object of joining the 6th Airborne Division as soon as possible, although 4 Commando was first to take Ouistreham.

The 4th Commando Brigade was split up as each unit had a separate task.

	Beach	Task
41 (RM) Cdo	Queen	Capture Lion-sur-Mer
46 (RM) Cdo	—	Capture Houlgate Battery
47 (RM) Cdo	Jig	Take Port en Bessin
Bde HQ and 48 (RM) Cdo	Nan	Attack Langrune-sur-Mer

Between Omaha and Gold there was a 10-mile gap. The British sector, between Port en Bessin and the River Orne, stretched for 24 miles.

At midnight on 6 June many of the D-Day objectives, notably Caen, were not as yet in British hands. On the other hand the Germans were far from achieving Rommel's aim of driving the invaders straight back into the sea.

Generally speaking, the seaborne landings were successful, which is not to say that everything went according to plan. However, one way and another, and despite the worst a determined enemy could do, every group managed sooner or later to carry out its task.

The most westerly objective of any British unit was Port en Bessin, the inter-Allied boundary. This was to be attacked by 47 (RM) Commando. They had a rough landing on Gold beach near St Côme de Fresne as the majority of their 16 landing craft were hit. As the first wave waded ashore they came under such heavy machine-gun fire that one marine is said to have remarked, 'Perhaps we're intruding. This seems to be a private beach.' The Commando suffered 43 casualties in the

Above: The gunshield of a US LST, manned by the Coast Guard, is repaired before the landings.
Left: Troopers of 13th/18th Hussars come ashore on 6th June.
Top: The minesweeper USS *Tide* sank on 7 June after hitting a mine off Omaha Beach.
Top right: American assault troops shelter beneath the cliffs at Colleville-Sur-Mer.
Right: A convoy of LCIs en route to the beachhead, protected by barrage balloons.

Left: Royal Marine commandos disembark from LCIs.
Right: The Mulberry artificial harbor at Arromanches provided a much-needed sheltered anchorage for supply ships.
Bottom right: The aftermath of the D-Day assault was a litter of broken vehicles and equipment and a row of corpses.
Below: A British casualty-clearing station positioned in the shelter of a sea wall.

landing. The rest concentrated at the back of the beach, and then set off westward across country. It had a sharp fight at La Rosière in the evening, but eventually reached Point 72, a prominent hill 1.5 miles south of their objective, where they dug in for the night. They attacked the little town of Port en Bessin next day, and with some fire support from HMS *Emerald* and three squadrons of rocket-firing Typhoons gradually overcame the opposition, though with heavy casualties. Eventually, at 0400 hours on 8 June, the garrison, still 300 strong, surrendered. The little harbor was put into immediate use, and proved of great value.

The 231st Brigade, veterans of the invasion of Sicily, landed on a two-battalion front. On their front the fortified village of Le Hamel was the main German strongpoint. This was still holding out when the second wave went in at about 0815 hours, and began to press toward Arromanches les Bains. The 1st Hampshire, the right assault battalion, lost its senior officers and progress was slow and costly. However the 1st Dorset swiftly took Les Roquettes and pushed inland. Flail tanks of the Westminster Dragoons and other Funnies landed punctually and set to work clearing mines and obstacles.

The 6th Battalion Green Howards of 69th Brigade made short work of a strongpoint at Hable de Heurtot and a battery position at Mont Fleury, whose gunners had been discouraged by bombing and by 12 direct hits from HMS *Orion*. In this fighting Sergeant Major S E Hollis won the Victoria Cross.

At La Rivière the 5th Battalion East Yorks was cornered by the sea wall, but naval gunfire and a flail from the Westminster Dragoons solved the problem. The tank knocked out an 88mm gun in its bunker

and 45 prisoners were taken. There followed a long, hard fight for the village, which cost 90 casualties. Two guns and 30 prisoners were taken in the strongpoint at the lighthouse near Mont Fleury. The battalion then pushed on inland toward Ver sur Mer. The 7th Battalion Green Howards passed through the assault battalions and took a battery beyond that village. It had been softened up by bombing and by HMS *Belfast*, and yielded 50 gunners, who had fired 87 rounds from their four 10cm gun howitzers, before losing heart.

The two assault brigade groups of the 50th Division, supported by DD tanks of the 4/7 Dragoon Guards and the Nottinghamshire Yeomanry were now pushing inland, and at about 1100 hours the 151st Brigade began to land over the beaches taken by the 69th Brigade. Le Hamel was still holding out, but by the early afternoon all four brigades of 50 Division were ashore. Since the oft-rehearsed counterattack of

the 915th German Infantry Regiment did not come to pass, progress was fairly satisfactory, although the 56th Brigade met with opposition outside Bayeux, which, however, fell next day.

The 3rd Canadian Division Group, who had not been in action before, landed a little late due to the rough weather. Most of their DD tanks got ashore, some of them ahead of the infantry. Effective covering fire from destroyers and support craft kept the Germans quiet until the landing craft touched down. The crews behaved with great resolution and valor, driving the larger landing craft on to the shore, and worming the smaller ones through the numerous obstacles as best they could. Ninety out of 306 landing craft employed by Force J were lost or damaged.

Courseulles, one of the main German positions on the Canadian front, held out stubbornly against the Regina Rifles, and there was fierce street fighting until well into the afternoon.

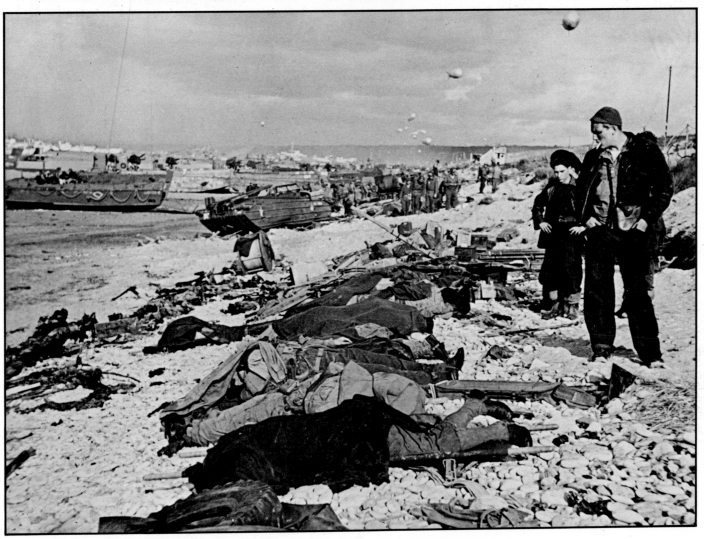

The Winnipeg Rifles, the reserve battalion of the 7th Canadian Brigade, avoided Courseulles and made good progress. They took Vaux and Ste Croix sur Mer.

Bernières, like Courseulles, was a hard nut to crack. The sea wall was 12 feet high in places, and behind it there were many fortified houses. Some had been demolished by naval gunfire, but the strongpoint was still a formidable one. Its infantry garrison had the support of two 50mm antitank guns, two heavy mortars and eight machine guns. The Queen's Own Rifles were enfiladed as they dashed across the beach, and suffered heavy losses. However, once they had outflanked the position by storming the sea wall, the defenders gave up. St Aubin sur Mer held out for three hours against the North Shore Regiment and assault engineers' tanks, and sniping went on until night fell.

By 1400 hours the whole Canadian Division was ashore: infantry, artillery and armor. The narrow strip of beach, uncovered by the rising tide, was choked with troops and vehicles, while damaged

landing craft littered the water's edge. Congestion on the beaches, and in Bernières, delayed the Canadians. When they tried to debouch into the open, undulating country beyond they were met by the fire of 88s and machine guns. Between Rivière and Bernières there were 11 antitank guns, belonging to the 716th Division, disposed across the path of the Canadians within a mile of the coast. Even so the 7th Canadian Brigade made good progress, taking Banville and Ste Croix sur Mer, and 'hordes of prisoners.' By 1600 hours they were across the Seulles. Three companies of the 726th Infantry Regiment had departed in disorder at their approach.

Near Fontaine-Henry the Regina Rifles, supported by tanks, came under heavy fire from 88s, but pushed on and took Le Fresne-Camilly.

The 8th Canadian Brigade took a battery 1000 yards west of Tailleville, bypassing another with 80 rockets, whose cables had been cut by the bombing so that they could not be fired. By 1430 hours, Bény sur Mer had fallen with 50 prisoners and a battery

of the 1716th Artillery Regiment (4 10cm guns) which had received more than 200 5.25-inch shells from HMS *Diadem*. At Tailleville a battalion HQ with a company of the 736th Grenadier Regiment held out in fortified houses connected by tunnels. It was late in the afternoon before the place was in the hands of the North Shore Regiment.

Thus the two leading Canadian brigades had advanced four or five miles inland. By 1430 hours the reserve brigade (9th) had made its way through Bernières and assembled south of the town. Its objective was Carpiquet, 10 miles away. It was not until after 1900 hours that the brigade reached Bèny sur Mer, though some of the North Nova Scotia Highlanders, lifted on tanks of the 27th Canadian Armored Regiment, arrived in the dusk at Villons les Buissons, after capturing some mortars and antitank guns. There was German armor, from 21st Panzer, between this force and the British 3rd Division. The Canadians were ordered to form a 'fortress' round the crossroads, where the road from Anisy to

Right: The Churchill was specially adapted to clear beach obstacles. The AVRE and flame-thrower versions gave especially good service on D-Day.
Below: The Sherman was the principal medium tank of the British and US armies. The amphibious version was extensively used on D-Day.

Above right: A Sherman with special air intakes for semisubmerged operations mired on a Normandy beach.
Right: Although obsolete as a fighting tank, the Valentine was used in the development of specialized obstacle-clearing AFVs.

Villons les Buissons crosses that from Courseulles to Caen.

Considering the congestion at Bernières the inexperienced but hardy Canadians did rather well on D-Day, though it is true that they were not counterattacked. Their armor had been particularly successful, knocking out a dozen or more of the dreaded 88s. Two troops of the 1st Hussars had actually reached the objective, the Bayeux–Caen road. However, they lacked infantry support and were compelled to fall back to their squadron.

The HQ of the 4th SS Brigade and 48 Commando encountered difficulties landing on Nan Beach (Juno) at about 0900 hours. Five of their six landing craft struck mines and one was hit by shellfire; two of them sank. A 'heavy swell and a vicious tidal stream . . . carried away and drowned men attempting to swim.' The beach defenses had survived the preliminary bombardment, but with the cover of a smoke screen the Commandos reached the cover of a low cliff and the sea wall, to find themselves among:

'a jumble of men from other units, including many wounded and dead; the beach was congested with tanks, heavy propelled guns and other vehicles . . . Tank landing craft were arriving all the time and attempting to land their loads, added to the general confusion.'

Y Troop, whose officers had become casualties, was taken back to England by a tank landing craft which had picked it up when its own craft had sunk. It was unable to rejoin its unit until two weeks later. Z Troop, some 40 strong, landed thanks to a stout-hearted leading seaman, who ferried men ashore in two lifts.

No 48 Commando, now only some 200 strong, took Langrune but was then held by a strongpoint near the shore. With the aid of a Sherman tank this was taken at about 1600 hours on 7 June. Two officers and 33 men of the 736th Grenadier Regiment laid down their arms. They had made a very creditable defense.

The 3rd Division, which Montgomery had commanded in the Dunkirk campaign, was the one with which he had first made his name. He never concealed his view that it was much better trained than the others in the BEF, and it had certainly proved itself a very useful formation. It must be said, however, that it was not really any better than other divisions, for example 1st and 4th, whose commanders were disinclined to publicize their exploits.

Since 1940 the 3rd Division had spent four years training in England, without any taste of active service. That it was thoroughly trained will be obvious. It may be that it had reached, and indeed passed, the point when it was overtrained. It is possible, though this is not a criticism which can be applied to *all* the units of the division, that it was a bit 'stale.'

The British 3rd Division, under Major General T G Rennie, was to attack on a front of one brigade. It landed on Queen Beach and spread out to cover the 2.5 miles between Lion sur Mer and Ouistreham. Both places were well fortified and about halfway between them was a strongpoint at La Brèche, bristling with wire,

Above: A German flak ship sunk in Port-en-Bessin harbor.
Right: A bulldozer demolishes defense works at Port-en-Bessin.

machine guns, mortars and the usual guns in casemates. The countryside was flat. On the north side of the coast road was a fairly high ridge of sand crowned with a more or less continuous row of houses.

The 8th Brigade landed on time and in the right place. Fire support was effective, but as the craft neared the shore the Germans opened up. Most of the DD tanks of the 13th/18th Hussars were launched at sea, and though 10 were knocked out in the surf, or soon after, 28 were left to support the infantry. The armored vehicles of the assault engineers landed with the leading wave and were the only supporting troops available from the very outset.

Here as elsewhere the crews of the landing craft showed the utmost determination. Of 18 craft that carried the self-propelled guns of the 7th, 33rd and 76th Field Regiments Royal Artillery, 14 became total wrecks; five from the effects of obstacles, three from mines and six from enemy fire. Miraculous though it may seem the 20 landing craft carrying the first infantry wave of 8th Brigade all got ashore without a casualty at 0730 hours. The leading companies of 1st South Lancashire and 2nd East Yorkshire Regiments began to attack the La Brèche strongpoint and to clear the houses along the dunes. 41 (RM) Commando (4th SS Brigade), which suffered heavy casualties on the beach, set off to attack Lion sur Mer. It made some progress, but the place was not finally subdued until next day, when a battalion of the Lincolnshire Regiment attacked it.

Along with two French troops of 10 (Inter-Allied) Commando, 4 Commando landed at 0820 hours on the heels of 8th Brigade, which they found 'pinned to the beach by intense fire.' The Commando passed through them, and took a pillbox which had been causing casualties. Then, led by the French troops under Commandant Kieffer, they moved against the

defenses of Ouistreham. A French gendarme, who met them, rendered invaluable service by pointing out the various German positions. After severe hand-to-hand fighting 4 Commando, with the support of four Centaur tanks from the Royal Marine Armored Support Regiment, took the Riva Bella battery, though not without heavy casualties.

A superb unit, 6 Commando, set off to blaze a trail inland and join hands with the 6th Airborne at the Bénouville bridge. 3 and 45 (RM) Commandos were to go in at H+90 and to follow 6 Commando. With the exception of 45 Commando, which was going into action for the first time, the 1st Commando Brigade was rather more experienced than most of the Allied troops who landed on D-Day. 4 Commando had stormed the Varengeville battery at Dieppe, 6 Commando had fought with great distinction in North Africa, and 3 had been at Vaagso, Dieppe, and the landings in Sicily and Italy.

Neither the La Brèche strongpoint nor Ouistreham had been subdued when at about 0900 hours the five landing craft infantry (LCI) carrying 3 Commando arrived 1000 yards from the beach and hove to within easy range of quite a number of German guns. They formed a line abreast with the precision worthy of a ceremonial parade.

53

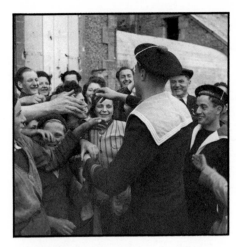

Above: French sailors from the invasion fleet in Port-en-Bessin.
Left: The Tricolor flies over Port-en-Bessin again.
Below: Commandos push inland from the beaches.
Bottom: 6th Royal Scots Fusiliers during the breakout from the beachhead.

The author of this book was commanding 3 Commando on this occasion. I was on the bridge of a landing craft talking to Lieutenant P Whitworth who commanded our division. The sea ran high, the weather was dull and gloomy, but the sight of HMS *Ramillies* belching 15-inch shells at the Bénerville battery was almost as good as a rum ration. A shell landed in the water 100 yards away and to port we could see a tank landing craft blazing; the crew were going over the side as the ammunition exploded. Battered houses along the shore looked vaguely familiar from the photographs we had been shown. Tanks were creeping about on the beach, but from in front of Ouistreham a German gun was firing at us every few seconds. This did not seem to be the time or the place to slow down. I asked Lieutenant Whitworth what he was waiting for.

'There are still five minutes to go before H+90,' he said with admirable sang froid.
'I don't think anyone will mind,' I replied, 'if we're five minutes *early* on D-Day.'
'Then in we go.'

Below: King George V shakes the hand of Lt Col Peter Young, who commanded No 3 Commando during the Normandy invasion.

We set off in a beautiful line, and not a moment too soon. Another shell. An airburst just ahead; the bits that reached us had lost all force. Then the next craft to starboard was hit, and seemed to shy like a horse. As we beached the gun at Ouistreham hit us and many of my men were up to their necks in water before they could struggle out of the hold.

The 4th division got all its five craft ashore, though three were hit and two completely wrecked. Such was the spirit of the RNVR, who put us ashore on D-Day. The commando lost about 30 men, mostly from the explosion of our own mortar bombs in one of the stricken craft. The first man ashore was Major J E Martin, our veteran administrative officer, who, as a trooper in the 9th Lancers, had had his baptism of fire on the Western Front in the year that I was born. He went right through – from Normandy to the Baltic.

There were quite a lot of infantry sitting about on the beach, and one cried out, 'Don't touch the bloody wire, it's mined.' We sorted ourselves out among the houses on the dunes, undisturbed except for a little indiscriminate mortar fire. Ahead lay 1000 yards of flat marshy meadow without a vestige of cover.

This, the first stage of our journey to the Bénouville bridges, was covered by a German quick-firing gun, but we survived its attentions more or less unscathed and pushed on to our forming-up place. Nearby we found a company commander of the assault brigade. He had his CSM (Company Sergeant Major) and two men with him. The rest, I rather thought, might be the men we had seen sitting on the beach.

La Brèche fell at about 1000 hours, after causing the assault brigade heavy casualties. The beaches were still under fire from guns inland, some of them beyond the Orne, but the 185th and 9th Brigades were able to come ashore during the morning and early afternoon. During the morning the 8th Brigade took Hermanville and Colleville and attacked two strongpoints, Morris and Hillman, a mile beyond. The first, which had suffered from air and naval bombardment, surrendered with 67 men and four field guns as soon as the attack began. The second, which was the well-sited HQ of 736th Regiment, held out until 2000 hours.

By about 1100 hours the infantry of 185th Brigade Group had assembled in woods about half a mile inland. Its vehicles, and heavy weapons, however, were held up by congestion on the beaches and by minefields. So at about 1230 hours the foot soldiers set off without them, reaching Périers ridge at about 1400 hours. Here they were joined by the leading tanks of the Staffordshire Yeomanry. There were German guns in the woods to their right, and these knocked out five tanks. They had to be ejected. The Staffordshire occupied a feature called Point 61, as a flank guard and base of fire, and the rest of the column moved on in the direction of Caen. It was some hours before the main body of the brigade got going. At 1500 hours 1st Battalion Royal Norfolk was ordered to secure high ground on the left of 2nd Battalion King's Shropshire Light Infantry. They thought St Aubin d'Arquenay was still in German hands, though in fact the Commando Brigade – including the present writer – went through it at about noon, making for Bénouville. Under this misapprehension the Norfolks moved through a large field, where, sadly, they soon lost 150 casualties to the machine guns of Hillman. It was not until 1900 hours that Beauville and Biéville were in British hands. The 2nd Battalion Royal Warwickshire, ordered to advance late in the afternoon, occupied St Aubin d'Arquenay at about 1800 hours – at least six hours after the Commandos had passed through. Opinions will differ as to whether this lack of urgency should be attributed to brigade or battalion.

Hesitation, at the highest level, afflicted the opposition. At 1432 hours Army Group B at last received permission – 12 hours after it had been requested – to move up 12th SS Panzer in support of Seventh Army. At 1507 hours authority was received to move Waffen SS 1 Panzer Corps and Panzer *Lehr* Division. General Dollmann (Seventh Army) ordered Lieutenant General Bayerlein (Panzer *Lehr*) to move on Caen at 1700 hours. The latter, with memories of the RAF in the Western Desert, urged that it was foolish to move before nightfall, but Dollmann, determined to attack at dawn on 7 July, would have none of this. Before Bayerlein and his HQ had passed Beaumont

sur Sarthe the bombs began to fall. A nightmare move followed, with Allied aircraft striking at every bottleneck on the five routes by which the long columns of vehicles were struggling to advance. Bayerlein wrote:

'At 2300 we drove through Sées. The place was lit up by flares hanging above it like candles on a Christmas tree, and heavy bombs were crashing down on the houses which were already burning. But we managed to get through.'

Meanwhile Feuchtinger had made his counterattack against 3rd Division. Under the continuous air attack requested by Dempsey, the 21st Panzer had crossed the Orne. By this time the 8th Brigade at Hermanville, Colleville sur Orne and Ouistreham was fairly well set, though 2nd Battalion East Yorkshire was occupied with a battery (Daimler) south of Ouistreham, and 1st Battalion Suffolk with the Hillman strongpoint. The 9th Brigade was assembling just inland of the beach, but was not yet ready to advance into the gap between the Canadians and Hermanville.

The main body of 185th Brigade was moving on Caen. The 2nd Battalion King's Shropshire Light Infantry (KSLI) with a squadron of tanks (Staffordshire Yeomanry) and some antitank guns, were at Beuville and Biéville. It must be said that KSLI seem to have had a real sense of the need to thrust forward on D-Day.

Soon after 1600 hours German tanks were reported moving up from Caen. A squadron supporting 1st Battalion Suffolk at Hillman was immediately moved to Biéville. No sooner had it taken up its position than 40 German tanks, moving very fast, came in from the west. The Staffordshire Yeomanry knocked out two with their 6-pounders. The rest sheared off into the woods. When they reappeared they suffered more casualties. Veering off once more, they were reinforced, and working round the right (western) flank approached the Périers ridge. They ran into the squadron, which had been positioned at Point 61 for just such an eventuality. The Germans lost three more tanks, and once again retired. They were now known by the British to have lost 13 tanks at a cost of one

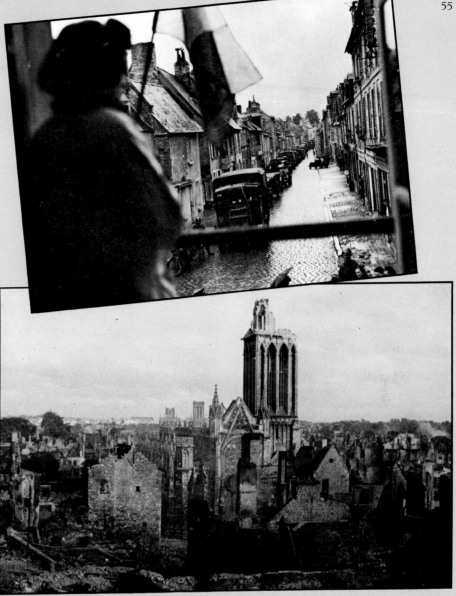

Above: This baby was born during the Allied bombardment of Caen.
Top left: A stretcher bearer of the Durham Light Infantry tends a wounded German soldier.
Left: A British sniper takes cover by the roadside at Tilly-sur-Seulles.
Top right: An Allied motor convoy winds through the narrow streets of Bayeux on its way to the front.
Right: The ruins of Caen after its capture on 9 July.

self-propelled gun. In fact Feuchtinger's losses were much heavier. According to him he began the day with 124 tanks, of which 54 were knocked out by nightfall. Eight Typhoons of the Second Tactical Air Force had accounted for six by dive bombing them on the outskirts of Caen. The division was nearly out of gasoline.

The repulse of 21st Panzer is very much to the credit of 3rd Division, and if they may be criticized for slowness, they deserve credit for their staunch conduct in the face of this dangerous counterattack.

The Commando Brigade joined hands with the 6th Airborne Division at about midday, the first commandos arriving on folding bicycles. Lovat sent them with all speed to relieve 9th Parachute Battalion and secure the Amfreville–Le Plein ridge, which overlooked the 3rd Division's area.

'We reached the bridges to find that they were under a desultory fire from a building perhaps 800 yards to the south. A group belonging to my bicycle troop were taking cover under the low bank to the left of the road.

I told them to get on their bikes and go across flat out. One was shot clean through the head. The rest got through. Now it was our turn, and we showed a very pretty turn of speed.

Lord Lovat came up, and told me that our planned move to Cabourg was off. We were to occupy Le Bas de Ranville so as to protect the HQ of the 6th Airborne Division and to block the German armor coming from the south. As we have seen the 21st Panzer did not turn up, which was just as well for we had not much in the way of antitank weapons. So we passed a peaceful afternoon in the June sunshine.'

At about 2100 hours some 240 gliders, towed by transport aircraft, came flying in low over the coast to land at Bénouville and Ranville. It was an astonishing sight. At a stroke the effective strength of the 6th Airborne Division was doubled. The reinforcements included two strong battalions and the reconnaissance regiment as well as some artillery. The effect on the morale of both sides was marked.

The telephone log of the German Seventh

Army records, 'Attack by the 21st Panzer Division rendered useless by heavily concentrated airborne troops.' Rommel's HQ was told that the 21st Panzer had 'been halted by renewed air landings.' The sight of this massed air landing taking place in their rear was naturally very discouraging to the Germans and led them to call off their counterattack. The Panzers fell back to a position between the KSLI and Caen. At midnight Seventh Army's signals diary summed up the situation in the Caen area:

'2400 hours. 716st Infantry Division is still defending itself at strongpoints. Communications between division, regimental and battalion headquarters, however, no longer exist, so that nothing is known as to the number of strongpoints still holding out or of those liquidated. . . . The Chief of Staff of Seventh Army gives the order that the counterattack of 7 June must reach the coast without fail, since the strongpoint defenders expect it of us.'

They were due for a disappointment.

6. A FATEFUL DAY

Why did the Allies win the battle of D-Day? Was Montgomery a greater general than von Rundstedt? Why did the Germans, with some 40 divisions at their disposal, get so many of them in the wrong places that the Allies were able to fight their way ashore, and stay there?

It must be remembered that in the first place the Allies had complete command in the air. In the second they had absolute command at sea. In the third, though Montgomery was not without fault he was probably a much better general than von Rundstedt, besides being more than a match for Rommel. He was, moreover, nobly supported by Bradley and Dempsey.

If the Allies had the advantage in the air and at sea, the Germans should have had a tremendous advantage on land, for they had far more divisions and, especially, many more Panzer divisions. Moreover their men were, on the whole, much more experienced than the Allies'. They were well led at every level.

The key point is that for one reason and another the German commanders were in two minds as to the significance of the reports that reached their headquarters. At 0215 hours Major General Pemsel reported to Rommel's Chief of Staff, General Speidel, 'the sound of engines can be heard coming from the sea on the eastern Cotentin coast . . . ,' and that Admiral, Channel Coast, reported the presence of ships in the sea area Cherbourg. To Pemsel all this activity indicated a major operation. Speidel did not agree and, more to the point, nor did von Rundstedt, who remained convinced that the main attack must come at Calais, and that therefore it had not yet begun.

Von Rundstedt was the key figure in the crisis, for Rommel was away. Keitel's opinion was neither here nor there, for had von Rundstedt been convinced that the genuine D-Day had arrived, one may suppose that the old Prussian warrior would have used his initiative and moved his reserves to where he thought Montgomery would least like to see them.

The most effective place to attack was Caen. A strong counterattack against the British left flank was the Germans' best chance of doing real damage on D-Day. As the campaign developed Montgomery expressed himself as being very well content to hold the mass of the German armor

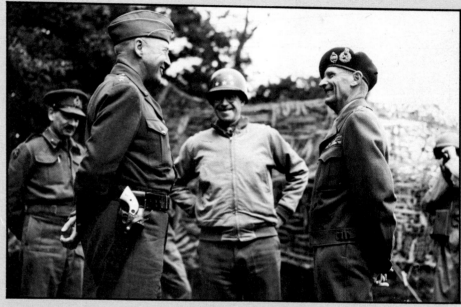

on the British front. However that may have been later on, a mass of German armor round Caen was the last thing the British wanted to meet on D-Day. Thanks to von Rundstedt's initial misapprehension there was only one Panzer division near enough to make itself felt early in the day. This was 21st Panzer under Lieutenant General Edgar Feuchtinger, an officer by no means lacking in initiative. His division was stationed at St Pierre sur Dives, only 15 miles from the coast. He had some 170 armored vehicles and tanks at his command. He has described the frustrations he suffered during the early hours of 6 June:

'I waited impatiently all night for some instructions. But not a single order from a higher formation was received by me. Realizing that my armored division was closest to the scene of operations, I finally decided at 0630 hours that I had to take some action. I ordered my tanks to attack the 6th Airborne Division which had entrenched itself in a bridgehead over the Orne. To me this constituted the most immediate threat to the German position.'

This was a shrewd and correct judgment, the more so as the 6th Airborne was very far from being entrenched by 0630, nor had it yet been reinforced by the commandos. Feuchtinger continues:

'Hardly had I made this decision when at 0700 hours I received my first intimation that a higher command did still exist. I was told by Army Group B that I was now under command of Seventh Army. But I received no further orders as to my role. At 0900 hours I was informed that I would receive any future orders from LXXXIV Infantry Corps (Marcks), and finally at 1000 hours I was given my first operational instructions. I was ordered to stop the move of my tanks against the Allied airborne troops, and to turn west and aid the forces protecting Caen.'

This was the crucial decision. Feuchtinger's armor, which had already been moving toward the coast 90 minutes before the first man of the British 3rd Division set foot ashore, was now condemned to spend the vital hours of D-Day in recrossing the single surviving bridge over the Orne at Caen. Had it carried out its original plan the 21st Panzer must have advanced via Le Bas de Ranville, which was held that afternoon by 3 Commando under the present author. An unpleasant situation would have occurred.

Another German commander who reacted quickly was General F Dollman, the commander of the Seventh Army. In the early hours of 6 June he gave orders for a three-pronged attack which, coming in from north, south and west, would crush

Above: Beachhead trenches were abandoned once the fighting moved inland.

Opposite: General George Patton, wearing his famous pearl-handled revolver, discusses the tactical situation with Bradley and Montgomery in early July.

Top left: The crew of a German 88mm gun in action. This famous weapon could be used against both tanks and aircraft.

Top right: The crew of a PzKpfw IV lie buried in front of their shattered tank in Normandy.

Above left: Axis troops manning this field gun include renegades from the Indian army enlisted by Germany from prisoners of war.

Left: Machine gunners of the Waffen SS keep watch for aircraft.

the American Airborne Divisions. Unfortunately for him, his divisional commanders had not got back from Rennes, where they had been attending an anti-invasion exercise. American soldiers and Resistance fighters alike had been busy cutting telephone lines, and several German commanders were simply unable to communicate with their Headquarters. Chaos and darkness was their lot, and that of their subordinates.

One of the best units in the Cotentin was the 6th German Parachute Regiment. It was decided to use it for the attack on the Americans between Carentan and Ste Mère Eglise, which has already been mentioned. Major Friedrich-August Freiherr von der Heydte collected his men, and then surveyed the scene from the tower of St Côme church. Six miles away he could see Utah, and found the sight 'overwhelming.' There, in the middle of the morning of D-Day, scores of landing craft were peacefully unloading in the sunshine. It was like 'Berlin Wannsee on a summer's afternoon.' The American airborne troops were nowhere to be seen.

Von der Heydte's first battalion broke through the scattered units of 101st Division without any difficulty, but his unit was cut in two by a follow-up landing of gliders and paratroops. The advance of US 8th Infantry Division from Utah spelled disaster for the 6th German Parachute Regiment, but they were not to know that until next day, 7 June.

At Omaha General Dietrich Kraiss, as we have seen, was convinced that his 352nd Division had stopped the Americans in their tracks. Reports from 716th Division were not so encouraging. The British were pressing toward Bayeux, where LXXXIV Corp's reserve, 915th Regiment, was stationed. This unit had practiced the counterattack toward the coast not once but many times. Now was the time to

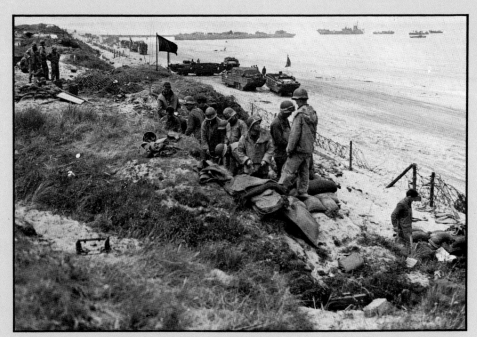

Above: Assault troops of the US 4th Infantry Division come ashore in full equipment.
Top left: LCVPs, pictured off the Normandy coast, were unarmored assault landing craft.
Top: A US Navy beach party takes over German-built trenches.
Left: LCTs were specially built as tank landing craft, but they carried many other vehicles.

carry it out in earnest. Imagine Kraiss' wrath when, at 0400 hours, he discovered that the 915th Regiment had been sent to Carentan to mop up the airborne landing! The General's reaction was to send a counterorder, which took an hour to get through. The troops – one may imagine their comments – turned about and moving on foot, on bicycles and in old French *camions* moved toward Omaha. However, one way and another they never managed to reinforce the defenders, who were gradually being winkled out of their bunkers. A veritable curtain of naval gunfire did much to prevent the replenishment of ammunition, which was essential if the Germans in the front line were to hold out. The counterattack of 915th Regiment came to nothing. A rather more dangerous onslaught was made by the 21st Panzer which, hampered by refugees, had made its way through Caen. The Allies were already in sight of the city with its tall cathedral when, late in the afternoon General Feuchtinger sent his armor in. He wrote:

'Once over the Orne river I drove north toward the coast. By this time the enemy . . . had made astonishing progress and had already occupied a strip of high ground about 10 kilometers from the sea. From here, the excellent antitank gunfire of the Allies knocked out 11 of my tanks before I had barely started. However, one battle group did manage to bypass these guns and actually reached the coast at Lion sur Mer, at about 1900 hours.'

This force, half a dozen tanks and a handful of infantry, was insufficient to turn the tide of battle. Indeed about three hours earlier the British had come up against the last tanks of the 21st Panzer counterattacking to save Caen. Before the Germans went into the attack General Marcks, with all the gravity he could muster, told their battalion commander, Colonel von Oppeln-Bronowski:

'Oppeln, the future of Germany may very well rest on your shoulders. If you don't push the British back we've lost the war.'

Nobody, who has not fought with and beaten the Germans, need trouble to boast of his soldiership! Yet for once these warwise warriors were taken by surprise. Rommel, for one, had been on leave. The storm in the Channel put the Germans off their guard. None of these things would have mattered had von Rundstedt's initial dispositions been correct. The Germans had a long tradition of expertise in land operations but von Rundstedt proved incapable of countering an amphibious operation. He should have seen that there were only two areas where the Allies could make their initial landfall. The obvious one was the Pas de Calais; the other was the one actually chosen, the area between the Orne and the Cotentin. A combination of

Below : The Mulberries enabled the speedy unloading of supplies for the front.

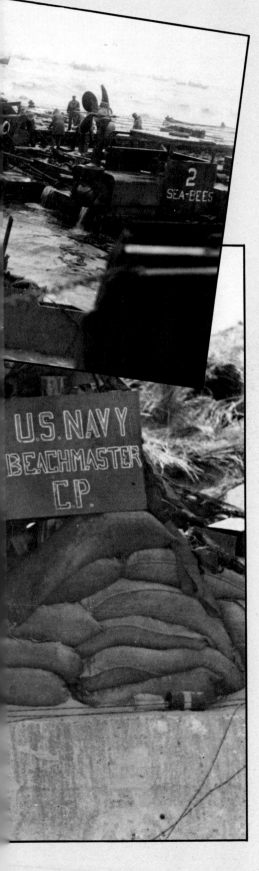

Bottom: Access to the beaches after D-Day was controlled and regulated by beachmasters.
Below: Without the shelter of artificial harbors, vessels were at the mercy of the elements, as these barges bear witness.

the two, though unlikely, was possible. It follows that the infantry in each of these areas should have been good quality, mobile divisions. Low grade static divisions were simply not good enough. In addition each of these two vital areas needed at least *two* Panzer divisions, one on each flank, and a Corps reserve of at least one more infantry division.

Field Marshal von Rundstedt, for all his service and experience, was baffled by the complexities of amphibious warfare. Even so it should not have been beyond his wit to work out that some parts of the coast were simply not going to be included in the Allies' beachhead area. One was the stretch of coast on either side of Dieppe, with its steep chalk cliffs and shingle beaches – especially after the fiasco of 1942. It follows that in this area the 84th Field Division could have been replaced by a low-category static formation.

Another area which was held with unnecessary strength was Brittany. There was no need for the 77th Division at St Malo, which could have been replaced by a static garrison. The same applies to the 353th Division as an Allied landing in Brittany was highly improbable. Not only was it much further from the ports of the south of England, it was too far from Paris, Antwerp and the other main objectives of any Allied campaign. Had von Rundstedt analyzed the situation more astutely and made a sounder allocation of his best divisions, it is possible that the Allies would have been repulsed on D-Day.

The D-Day battle fell naturally into three phases. The first was the breaking of the Atlantic Wall, the second was the thrust inland, and the third was the consolidation in order to repel the inevitable counterattack.

The first phase, despite initial setbacks at Omaha, was everywhere remarkably successful. The Atlantic Wall, for all the skill that had gone into its construction, proved a great deal less formidable than expected. Or, to put it another way, the Allied troops, and particularly the British and Canadians, came trained and equipped to deal with every sort of obstacle. This is perhaps the place to pay tribute to Major General Sir Percy Hobart, whose 'funny' tanks loaded the dice in favor of the British infantryman.

Progress made in the second phase of the D-Day fighting was disappointing, in that Caen, Bayeux and St Lô were still in German hands when night fell. It must be remembered that the planners were bound to be optimistic in selecting their objectives for D-Day. Complete success was not perhaps to be looked for from troops who, after a night spent being seasick in ships and landing craft, had already stormed the West Wall. Credit must go to those, including 6th Airborne and the commandos, who actually attained most of their objectives.

In any big amphibious operation it is essential at the outset to capture enough ground to give the force room to maneuver. Experience shows that one can capture terrain on D-Day which thereafter can only be taken at heavy cost, because the enemy has had time to organize defenses. It therefore behooves the advancing troops to take risks on D-Day, to get a move on. It cannot be said that all the Allied troops engaged bore this in mind. Some, it must be said, were decidedly cautious. It was rather unfortunate for the British that the 21st Panzer appeared on the front of a division which had been trained to plod forward at 100 yards in three minutes, covered by massive artillery fire. Tactics appropriate enough for a set-piece battle were not necessarily the best answer for the fluid situation met with on D-Day.

The consolidation phase was something which the Allied commanders at every level thoroughly understood. They were quick to dig in and secure the ground they had gained. Thanks to such imaginative devices as the Mulberry harbor and PLUTO (Pipeline Under The Ocean) the administrative buildup put the Army Group on a sound footing in good time before, on 19 June, the worst storm in the Channel for more than 40 years struck the Assault Area.

Many years have passed since the Allies won this astonishing victory. It is not likely that the world will see such another, for a single nuclear weapon in the assault area might suffice to bring the whole amphibious machine to a disastrous halt. It is a solemn thought.

Yet, if it is no longer possible to contemplate an operation of this kind, it is worth pausing for a moment to recall the magnitude of the effort which the Allies put forth on 6 June 1944. Allied aircraft flew 14,000 sorties during the night of 5 June and on D-Day. In these operations 127 aircraft were lost and 63 damaged.

More than 195,000 men were engaged in the ships and craft taking part in the naval operations. Over 23,000 airborne troops, about 8000 British and 15,500 American, were landed from the air. Total American casualties were 6000.

In the British Sector the airborne troops and commandos had about 1300 casualties, including 100 glider pilots. Casualties among the seaborne troops were some 3000, of whom about 1000 were Canadians. Thus 156,215 troops were landed, from sea and air, in Normandy, and at a cost of some 10,300 casualties, broke Hitler's Atlantic Wall in a single day.

To one who had fought at Dunkirk and Dieppe it did seem that – at long last – our side had managed to get itself organized. In four years we had invented and mastered the intricate techniques of amphibious warfare. The road from the beaches of Normandy to the shores of the Baltic was a long one, and few indeed were to go the whole way. Still, they had got off to a good start.

APPENDIX

US D-Day Assault Divisions

OMAHA BEACH

1st US Division
116 Infantry
16 Infantry
18 Infantry
26 Infantry
115 Infantry
2nd Rangers
5th Rangers
741 Tank Battalion
111 Field Artillery Battalion
7 Field Artillery Battalion
81 Chemical Battalion

UTAH BEACH

4th US Division
8 Infantry
22 Infantry
12 Infantry
359 Infantry (attached from 90th Division)
70 Tank Battalion

British D-Day Assault Divisions

SWORD BEACH

3rd British Division
8th Brigade
1st Battalion The Suffolk Regiment
2nd Battalion The East Yorkshire Regiment
1st Battalion The South Lancashire Regiment
9th Brigade
2nd Battalion The Lincolnshire Regiment
1st Battalion The King's Own Scottish Borders
2nd Battalion The Royal Ulster Rifles
185th Brigade
2nd Battalion The Royal Warwickshire Regiment
1st Battalion The Royal Norfolk Regiment
2nd Battalion The King's Shropshire Light Infantry
Divisional Troops
3rd Reconnaissance Regiment RAC
3rd Divisional Engineers
3rd Divisional Signals
7th, 33rd and 76th Field, 20th Antitank and 92nd Light Antiaircraft Regiments RA
2nd Battalion The Middlesex Regiment (Machine Gun)

JUNO BEACH

3rd Canadian Division
7th Brigade
The Royal Winnipeg Rifles
The Regina Rifle Regiment
1st Battalion The Canadian Scottish Regiment
8th Brigade
The Queen's Own Rifles of Canada
Le Régiment de la Chaudière
The North Shore (New Brunswick) Regiment
9th Brigade
The Highland Light Infantry of Canada
The Stormont, Dundas and Glengarry Highlanders
The North Nova Scotia Highlanders
Divisional Troops
7th Reconnaissance Regiment (17th Duke of York's Royal Canadian Hussars)
3rd Canadian Divisional Engineers
3rd Canadian Divisional Signals
12th, 13th and 14th Field, 3rd Artillery and 4th Light Antiaircraft Regiments, RCA
The Cameron Highlanders of Ottawa (Machine Gun)

GOLD BEACH

50th British (Northumbrian) Division
69th Brigade
5th Battalion The East Yorkshire Regiment
6th and 7th Battalion The Green Howards
151st Brigade
6th, 8th and 9th Battalions The Durham Light Infantry
231st Brigade
2nd Battalion The Devonshire Regiment
1st Battalion The Hampshire Regiment
1st Battalion The Dorsetshire Regiment
Divisional Troops
61st Reconnaissance Regiment RAC
50th Divisional Engineers
50th Divisional Signals
74th, 90th and 124th Field, 102nd Antitank and 25th Light Antiaircraft Regiments, RA
2nd Battalion The Cheshire Regiment (Machine Gun)

Other Formations

79th Armored Division
30th Armored Brigade
22nd Dragoons
1st Lothians and Border Horse
2nd County of London Yeomanry (Westminster Dragoons)
141st Regiment RAC
1st Tank Brigade
11th, 42nd and 49th Battalions RTR
1st Assault Brigade RE
5th, 6th and 42nd Assault Regiments RE
79th Armored Division Signals
1st Canadian Armored Personnel Carrier Regiment
1st Special Service Brigade
Nos 3, 4 and 6 Commandos
No 45 (Royal Marine) Commando
4th Special Service Brigade
Nos 41, 46, 47 and 48 (Royal Marine) Commandos
Royal Marine
Armored Support Group: 1st and 2nd Royal Marine Armored Support Regiments
Units of the Royal Artillery and Royal Engineers

Airborne Forces

6th Airborne Division

3rd Parachute Brigade
8th and 9th Battalions The Parachute Regiment
1st Canadian Parachute Battalion
5th Parachute Brigade
7th, 12th and 13th Battalions The Parachute Regiment
6th Airlanding Brigade
12th Battalion The Devonshire Regiment
2nd Battaltion The Oxfordshire and Buckinghamshire Light Infantry
1st Battalion The Royal Ulster Rifles
Divisional Troops
6th Airborne Armored Reconnaissance Regiment RAC
6th Airborne Divisional Engineers
53rd Airlanding Light Regiment RA
6th Airborne Division Signals

US 101st Airborne Divisions

501st Parachute Infantry
502nd Parachute Infantry Regiment
506th Parachute Infantry
377th Parachute Field Artillery Battalion

US 82nd Airborne Division

505th Parachute Infantry
507th Parachute Infantry
508th Parachute Infantry

INDEX

Acknowledgments
The author would like to thank the
following individuals who helped prepare
this book:

Jane Laslett, the editor
Adrian Hodgkins, the designer
Anthony Robinson for writing the captions
Richard Natkiel for supplying the maps
Penny Murphy for preparing the index

Picture Credits
The author would also like to thank the individuals
and agencies listed below for the use of their
artwork and photographs:

Graham Bingham (artwork): pp 50 (both),
51 (bottom)
Bison: pp 6 (top right and bottom), 9 (top),
10 (below), 11 (top), 12 (top), 14 (both), 17, 37 (top),
48 (below), 49 (top), 57 (center right)
Bundesarchiv: pp 6 (top left), 8, 57 (top left and
bottom)
Robert Hunt: pp 13 (bottom), 20 (bottom two),
24 (top), 25 (top), 26–27, 28 (bottom), 33, 48 (top),
49 (bottom), 52 (top two and center), 53 (top),
55 (all three), 57 (center left)
Imperial War Museum: pp 1, 9 (below), 10 (top),
13 (bottom), 18, 20 (main pic), 21, 29, 53
(center and bottom), 54 (both), 57 (top right),
60 (center)
National Archives: pp 18 (top), 32 (bottom), 35 (all
three), 36–37 (bottom), 39 (bottom), 40 (top), 40–41
(bottom), 41 (top), 42 (top), 44–45 (bottom),
46 (center and top), 47 (top), 51 (top),
58 (both), 59 (top), 60 (top and bottom)
Peter Young: p 53 (right)
US Army: pp 12 (center), 15 (both), 24 (center),
28 (top two), 34 (bottom), 36 (top), 38 (all three),
39 (top), 42–43 (bottom), 43 (bottom), 44 (top left),
47 (bottom), 56, 59 (center)
US Air Force: pp 19, 25 (bottom), 30 (both), 32 (top)
US Coast Guard: p 44 (top right)
US Navy: pp 4–5, 16, 40 (center), 46